ANGELS IN MY HAND

KARL MILLER

Library of Congress Control Number: 1999454879
ISBN: 978-0-615-26788-3

To: Brittany & John David

THANK YOU...

To my wonderful family, who gave me their love and support
during the writing of this book—my wife Barb, my daughters
Angie and Lindsey, and my sons-in-law, Jon and Dean.

To Jack Snader for his help in making this happen. This
book would not be possible without his gift of writing
and his determination to put my stories on paper.

To my many friends, who, over the years, encouraged
me to write a book about my angel ministry.

To everyone who keeps me supplied with coffee can lids.

In memory of my parents, Abram and Dorothy, my sister Janie, and my brother Ken, who are with the Lord in Heaven. I would not be where I am today without witnessing their example of faith and dedication to prayer.

Contents

Introduction

Before I formed you in the womb I knew you, before you were
born I set you apart; I appointed you as a prophet to the nations.
Jeremiah 1:5 (NIV)

I make angels out of coffee can lids, and then I give them away. It sounds like a simple thing, but God has led me to a special ministry, and the results of a seemingly simple mission have been bountiful beyond belief.

I didn't wake up one day and decide to start making angels. In fact, the thought of speaking to strangers about anything, let alone God and what Jesus Christ has done for us, was a completely unfamiliar notion for the first 30 years of my life. But God took time to prepare me. His tools were varied, but they always hit the mark. He guided me away from a dark, unknown road and let me watch the sun rise on a brand new life.

Listening to God is like tuning in a radio station. The static crackles as we scan the dial, trying to figure out what God wants us to do. Finally a station comes in clear and strong. God is playing the music, but it doesn't seem quite right. We know what God is asking of us, but it's too much to ask, or so we think, so we turn the dial again. We want songs that perfectly fit our comfortable lives, but God asks us to step outside our comfort zones. He asks us to take risks and dance to the beat of His music, not spend a lifetime searching for stations.

The fear is not so much taking the first risk, but knowing God won't be satisfied with it. We're afraid of what He'll ask us to do next. Yes, the first steps are hard, but like a runner training for a race, each day gets easier, the strides become longer, and the miles fly by faster. We build confidence with practice and character with action. We run the race on faith and deeds, and when we run the race we feel strong and blessed. The pitfalls and bleak times strengthen us and that is when we need our faith to let God pull us through our trials.

God has seized my soul and led me on exciting and enlightening journeys, although I have not always been a willing traveler. I have made many mistakes, and I will most likely make more. But God pursues me and loves me, and I can never again tune the radio to a different station. He has used angels throughout my life to guide and shape me, and He has used me to shape angels and give them wings to fly into the hearts and souls of others. I now give out more than 200 angels every year, and what God has done for me, He can and will do for anyone.

I am nobody special. I have never seen an angel, but I know people who have. I have yet to see the Gates of Heaven, but I have seen heavenly miracles on earth. It took me a long time to begin to listen to what God had to say to me. Now I want to share the story of how my ministry began, and my joy in what God has done for me and what He has allowed me to do for others.

I
Beginnings

The Father hears you when you pray
Anytime, night or day
And He will say
I'm watching with angels
I'm ready to fly
One word, just a whisper
I'll be there
Knock and He'll open
Seek and you'll find
Call on His name, He's the answer
Waiting for a prayer.

Natalie Grant

A Mother's Prayer

I have no greater joy than to hear that
my children are walking in the truth.
III John 1:4 (NIV)

I never knew my father. I was eight weeks old and in the hospital for a hernia operation when he died of a heart attack at age 39. My mom had to cope with the loss of her spouse, a frail infant and two older children. Her faith is what kept her grounded. Through all of her trials, she never stopped praying. My mom taught me the importance of prayer.

I grew up in a Christian home on a 13-acre farm in Lancaster, Pennsylvania. My mom, brother, sister and I went to church every week. My mom prayed for her children daily. I needed those prayers while I was growing up. She prayed me through my delicate infancy. Doctors gave up on me, but she never did. She prayed for me when I was a young child and adolescent. I went to church, but it didn't make me a perfect kid. She prayed me through my teens and young adulthood, as I often strayed far from the narrow road. She prayed me through my cross-country motorcycle trips. She prayed me through my hard-partying nights.

She must have prayed for me to meet a woman who would encourage me to begin a closer walk with God, because that's exactly what happened. I met Barb at a dance and I soon realized it was more than her long, blonde hair and blue eyes I was attracted to. She was easy to talk to, sensitive and caring. We had similar backgrounds. Most importantly, she was a Christian. Even though I had drifted from my Christianity, I always wanted to marry a Christian woman. After dating for three years, we married in 1978. Our first daughter, Angie, was born in 1981, and Lindsey followed in 1983. We were thrilled to be parents, and becoming a father brought me much joy and happiness.

Since my father died when I was young, it was always important to me to be the best dad I could be to my daughters. I thought my life was set. My mom's prayers must have paid off. I had sowed my wild oats and I now had a wonderful family, and all seemed right with the world. But my mom continued to be a major factor in my life.

One evening in March of 1983, as my mom was watching television, she fell asleep and entered Heaven. A massive heart attack took her life at 67. I know I'm not the first person to be angry with God, and I'm not the first person to be frustrated and want to know why things happen, but she was the only parent I had ever known. She was a pillar in my life, and a piece of my heart was torn away when she died.

I inherited my Christianity from my mom. As long as she was living, maybe I didn't have to search my soul. I had my mom praying for me. So far, her prayers had been enough, and I had done well. But God does not let us inherit our Christianity. We have to find it on our own, and my search was only beginning. There was no indication her death would affect me in so many ways.

Rain was in the forecast for the day of my mom's funeral. I prayed to God, "Lord, if you're up there, the least you can do is have it not rain for the service. My mom deserves at least that much."

That night I heard and felt God's Spirit, a voice—ethereal, earthly and eerie—all rolled into one. God's voice told me it would not rain for the funeral, but the sky would open up later that night to give me a glimpse of God. The lightning and thunder to come would shake my very soul. I woke Barb and told her what God had told me, hoping she wouldn't think I was crazy.

Early the morning of the funeral, God surprised me again. Angie, my daughter, woke up calling, "Daddy, daddy," in a soft, sweet voice. She never called for me before, she always called for Barb. But she kept calling, "Daddy, daddy." Wiping away a few tears, thinking about both my mom and daughter, I went to Angie in her crib. She stood angelically with her arms open wide. So far, her speech had been limited to very simple sentences, so when she said, "Don't cry Daddy. I love you," I was speechless. Then she hugged me with a hug that was not of a 2-year-old. I felt arms wrap around me like an adult. It was a hug, a feeling, a touch from God himself, and it will stay with me forever.

It was an ugly, windy, raw day. Rain threatened every moment of the funeral, but not one drop fell. "OK Lord," I thought, "I should have asked for sunshine, not a day without rain." But God was giving me what I asked for, and I was still too upset to notice.

After the service, a former Sunday school teacher came up to me and said, "Hey Karl, I thought it was going to rain at the cemetery for your mom's service, didn't you?'

"Yeah," I replied.

"But it didn't rain did it?"

"No, it didn't," I said, surprised.

"Isn't that amazing? It's a miracle it didn't rain," he said, with a smile on his face. He had no idea what I had prayed for and what God told me was going to happen.

I couldn't figure out if God was using this man to get my attention, poke fun at me, or if He thought I was so thick-headed that I needed a few more signs. God whispers to some people, and they hear His voice and follow Him. Some people need a gentle nudge in the right direction.

But there are those people who need to be shaken by the very Hand of God at the crossroads in their life. That would be me. The lack of rain, Angie, my former Sunday school teacher—it wasn't enough. I was faced with a crisis in my life, and I still didn't know who to turn to.

When we got home from the funeral, I was still feeling frustrated, sad, and disappointed. The day had drained me. I dozed off but God was about to change my life forever. Lightning flashed like a million cameras taking pictures from every angle. Thunder jolted the house like an earthquake, and the rain came down like a waterfall from Heaven. I was petrified. My soul was laid bare. Lying in my bed with my eyes wide open, I knew I could no longer doubt God. For the first time, I knew I had a purpose in life. Finally, I heard His voice. Now what was God going to do with me? Although I knew my mom was still praying for me, I also knew, from that moment on, I had to start carving my own relationship with God. I was also about to find out my mom's death would affect me as much as her life did.

My mom passed away a few days before Easter. That year, Barb and I hosted our family Easter gathering. The main topic of conversation, of course, was our mom. We passed stories around the table along with the ham and mashed potatoes. We laughed and cried over all the memories. My sister, Janie, told a story I had never heard before. Obviously, God wanted me to hear it now. Had I heard it earlier in my life, it wouldn't have meant as much to me.

Several years before I was born, my parents and Janie, who was nine years old at the time, were standing on our front porch. The willow tree down near the chicken house was swaying in the breeze. Looking towards the tree, my mom and sister saw the sky part a bit, and puffy white clouds formed a circle. My mom looked at the circle of clouds and exclaimed, "Look, there are angels in the sky! Do you see them?"

By the look on my sister's face, my mom knew she had seen them, too.

"Yes," Janie replied, "I see them. I really do."

"What are you talking about?" my father asked. "I don't see any angels."

"Don't you see the angels? Don't you see them?" my mom and sister both asked him.

"No, I don't see anything but clouds," he said, in a discouraged tone.

The angel vision was real. God knew my mom and sister would need reassurance. God, in His magnificent plan, also knew I would need this story to comfort me at some point in my life. My sister, though very young, had no doubt about what she saw. She had a fascination with angels for several years after the vision. She started collecting angels and putting them on the walls, but when they started ruining the wallpaper, my mom had to put a stop to it.

My mom and sister never completely understood the vision. It strengthened their faith, and it gave them the peace and reassurance they would need to face the challenges to come. My mom would become a widow and have to raise three children on her own, but she always knew she had angels watching over her. And for me, perhaps the vision was a harbinger of things to come.

. . .If any want to become my followers, let them deny themselves and take up their cross and follow me. For those who want to save their life will lose it, and those who lose their life for my sake will find it. For what will it profit them if they gain the whole world but forfeit their life? Or what will they give in return for their life?
Matthew 16:24-26 (NRSV)

Godly sorrow brings repentance that leads to salvation and leaves no regret. . .
2 Corinthians 7:10 (NIV)

The Find of a Lifetime

How can young people keep their way pure?
By guarding it according to your word.
Psalms 119:9 (NRSV)

*I*n the weeks following my mom's death, we had to sort through her belongings and decide what would go to the auction and what would be divided among the children. Childhood memories came flooding back as I wandered around the house. I was drawn to my room, which looked exactly the same as when I was younger. In a drawer, I found one of two gifts she'd given to me for graduating high school. It was a watch I had never been able to wear because it irritated my wrist whenever I put it on.

As I sat on the bed and looked around, I saw a stack of dusty books. Buried among them was the other graduation gift from my mom, a Living Bible that had never been opened. The pages still crinkled with crispness as I leafed through it. My mom wanted me to read it, but I had things to do and places to go. I went to church, but the Bible stayed on the shelf.

As I held the Bible in my hands, I felt the urge to hang on to it like a baby hangs on to its pacifier. I didn't want to put it down. The first morning I went back to work, I tucked my Bible under my arm and headed out the door.

"Are you taking your Bible to work?" Barb asked me.

"Yes, I have a few breaks, and an hour for lunch. I want to keep reading," I told her.

I am thankful God encouraged me to read the New Testament first. In two weeks, I had finished it. I finished the entire Bible in about four months, every word of it. I felt like angels were turning the pages for me, helping me to mark and copy every special verse.

The angels must have been turning my pastor's pages, too. Every Sunday in church, he used scripture from exactly where I was reading at the time. Once or twice could be a coincidence, but this was happening every week. One week was particularly astounding. The pastor was not even close to where I was reading. He was wrapping up the sermon, and I thought, "OK, Lord, after all these weeks, don't stop now. Did I make a mistake?"

But sure enough, the pastor ended by saying he wanted to leave us with a verse from Matthew 24:31, "And he will send his angels with a loud trumpet call, and they will gather his elect from the four winds, from one end of the heavens to the other." It was exactly where I was reading.

I marked different passages in my Bible and I copied my favorite verses, but reading the Bible did not make me a scholar on religion. Quite frankly, there was a lot in the Bible I didn't understand as I read through it the first time. There will be a lot I won't completely understand when I read it for the 100th time, but if anyone picks up a Bible and reads it, God will use it to influence his or her life. The Bible, the Book of Life, the road map to Heaven, will teach us to search out God's face and His glory. Too often, we search for God's hand, asking for His help, instead of reading the Bible and searching for His radiance to help us shine.

Since reading the Bible was important to me, God led me to purchase Bibles for the fourth-graders in our church. I wanted each child's name imprinted on the cover so the Bibles would be personalized. I realized this would be a relatively expensive investment, but God gave me a peace that He would meet my needs. That year, a group of my co-workers and I were working on a special project that we finished under budget and on time. We each received an unexpected bonus. After taxes, the amount of the bonus was the exact amount I had paid for the Bibles. It was not a coincidence. It was God's way of reassuring me. As long as I took the time to listen and obey, He would provide. We can never out-give God. For more than 15 years I purchased the Bibles, and every year God, unfailingly, provided.

I had one more opportunity to visit my mom's house the year she passed away. We rented it to a family for the summer, and when they moved out I checked to make sure the water was turned off and it was locked. As I entered the empty house, I could still visualize my mom's furniture in its place. I breathed in the memories. Upstairs, I was drawn to the bedroom where my mom had passed away. As I walked closer, I noticed a piece of paper stuck to the door, and I was surprised to see it was a child's drawing of an angel. The only thing left in the house was an angel taped to the door of the room where my mom passed away. Apparently, a child who lived there put the picture on the door, but I knew it was for me. I knew I was supposed to have that angel. With tears, I remembered the story my sister shared about their angel vision. Carefully, I took the treasure off the door. I knew what to do with it. I taped it inside the cover of my Bible, the same one my mom gave me years before. It's still there today. The Bible is worn and ragged, but the angel looks as fresh as the day I put it there. I knew the angel was special; God led me through more experiences to find out just how special it was.

My mom is smiling in heaven. She was never able to see the fruits of half her prayers. Now she was beginning to reap what she had sown, and through reading the Bible, I was beginning to understand her prayers and figure out what she had done for me. Her prayers were like the hard shell of a seed, protecting and preparing me for the Lord's service. As the shell wore through, I had to root my own spiritual life on that same principle of prayer. Through droughts and floods, my seed struggled and grew, and those prayers are what eventually led me to my ministry through angels. Early in my walk with Jesus, when I was taking baby steps, God gave me the experience of finding the angel drawing, which helped my steps become stronger and truer. It's all about God's timing.

Some give freely, yet grow all the richer; others withhold what is due, and only suffer want. A generous person will be enriched, and one who gives water will get water.
Proverbs 11:24-25 (NRSV)

The angel I found on my mom's door.

Time is Ticking Away

If we confess our sins, he is faithful and just and will forgive
us our sins and purify us from all unrighteousness.
1 John 1:9 (NIV)

When I was in the fourth grade, I stole a watch from a girl, a classmate of mine. It was not the worst thing I have done, but it was an event that took up residence in a part of my brain and troubled me for 20 years. I was about to experience how God works in mysterious ways.

I was becoming stronger in my faith, but I felt like a tiny sponge trying to suck up the Atlantic Ocean. A seminar led by Bill Gothard, the founder of the Institute in Basic Life Principles, turned out to be one of the most important learning experiences in my walk with God.

He said something at the seminar that made quite an impression on me: if we had a blot on our conscience, we should try to clear it away. To do this we should meet face-to-face with the person we transgressed and make it right. The person may not forgive us, but God will. Prayer would give us the strength we needed. Prayer would even bring that person across our path.

After 20 years, the watch was still a blot on my conscience. In years past I had seen this girl, now a woman, around town, but we had not spoken since we were in school together. I felt too ashamed to acknowledge her, hoping I could forget what happened. I had not seen her for quite a while, but finally, I had the tools I needed to heal this wound. For the first time, I wanted to see her again. I prayed for our paths to cross. I prayed at home. I prayed at work. My stomach churned with anticipation, and I had doubts about ever seeing this woman again, but I prayed with all the faith I could muster. This act of prayer would be a defining moment in my life.

A few days after the seminar, I was sitting outside on a bench over my lunch hour. I had finished praying, and I was wondering if I would ever see this woman. At that moment, something surreal happened. Across the street, walking with a child, I saw her. It was a miracle. With the speed of an Olympian and guardian angels at my side, I darted across the busy city street. Slightly out of breath, I caught up to her.

"I don't know if you remember me," I said. "I'm Karl Miller. I've been praying I would meet up with you, and I am so happy my prayers were answered. I took your watch in fourth grade, and I have regretted it ever since. I wanted to let you know how sorry I am."

"I remember someone taking my watch, but I never knew who it was," she replied, surprised and confused.

"Here, please take this," I said, as I grabbed for my wallet and gave her all the cash I had.

"I can't take your money. That was years ago," she said.

"Please take it," I said. "I'm really sorry. I shouldn't have taken your watch."

She hurried off and I turned to go back to work. A combination of feelings surged through me, amazement that God had allowed me to meet her after so many years, and relief the burden of the watch was lifted. It showed the power of God, and the power of prayer.

That evening, I searched my drawer to find the watch my mom gave me for graduation, the watch I could never wear because it irritated my wrist. With tears in my eyes, I slipped it on my wrist. There was no irritation. It felt like a warm glove on a cold winter's day. I could finally wear it. It was a small symbol of all my mom had done for me. A watch, a symbol of fleeting time, would become one of my answers to prayer later in my life. It would become a major part of my ministry in years to come. I didn't know then how truly important this event was in my life, but I felt a peace I never felt before.

A few days later, I was catching my last fly ball during softball practice for the church team. I looked down, and there, laying in center field, was a brand new $20 bill. There were no creases, crinkles or folds. It looked hot off the press. I picked it up and ran towards the bench where everyone was cleaning up and getting ready to go home.

"Who lost a twenty in the outfield?" I yelled.

Everyone checked their wallets, but no one was missing any money.

"Must be yours, Karl. Finders, keepers," one guy laughed.

"I can't keep this. Come on, I'll buy everyone ice cream."

"No," they said, "just keep it, Karl."

The next day at work, I told my boss about the $20 bill, and how it was so new, like an angel had laid it there for me. With a thoughtful look on his face, he said, "Karl, you must have done a good deed recently."

Then it hit me...the watch! I bet I gave the woman $20. I have no way of knowing for sure, but God, in his own humorous way, was giving my money back to me for being obedient, taking a risk and trusting in Him. God had already forgiven me.

II.
Growth

An angel can illumine the thought and mind of man by strengthening the power of vision, and by bringing within his reach some truth which the angel himself contemplates.

St. Thomas Aquinas

After I had read the Bible and I had found the power of prayer, I was on top of the mountain. My cup was full. The adrenaline was pumping as if I was a skydiver waiting to jump, but where was I supposed to land? I had my dancing shoes on, and I was ready to dance with Jesus, but I did not know whether to do the two-step or the tango, the waltz or the twist. God had a mission for me; I just did not know what it was. Jesus had fed me the Word, and for the first time in my life I knew how small I really was, and how much God wanted me to grow. God would never give me more than I could handle, but there were some trips down the mountainside yet to come. A lot happened in the years after my mom's death.

Mountains High and Valleys Low

So Elijah fled for his life. . . he went on alone into the wilderness, traveling all day, and sat down under a broom bush and prayed that he might die.

"I've had enough," he told the Lord. "Take away my life. I've got to die sometime, and it might as well be now."

Then he lay down and slept. . . but as he was sleeping, an angel touched him and told him to get up and eat! He looked around and saw some bread baking on hot stones, and a jar of water!. . . So he got up and ate and drank, and the food gave him enough strength to travel forty days and forty nights to Mount Horeb, the mountain of God.

1 Kings 19:3-8 (TLB)

*G*od was beginning to take me, a lowly lump of clay, and mold me anew. After all, He gave me a new life, and I already had a wonderful family. I found the presence of God. I could handle sacrificing some small things for God. I did not, however, handle everything quite so easily.

A few days before Easter in April 1987, Barb came to work to tell me my brother, Ken, had died of a massive heart attack while he was sitting in the doctor's office. He had gone there complaining of chest pains. He was only 39 years old, the same age my father had been when he died. It shook me. I was finally accepting my mom's death four years earlier when God took my older brother, my best friend. Because I grew up without my father, Ken was very important to me. We had fun raising pigeons and even raising a little, well, trouble. He was too young, and he left a family just as my dad had.

I was angry and frustrated, and I prayed in anger and frustration. God wants us to do that. He wants to hear our cries and our sorrows, and He wants to soothe us. I had my Bible and I prayed, "Lord, I need some answers, and I need them now. Not in one year or two years, but right now. You took my father and mother, and now my brother. All I have left is my sister. You have to lead me to a scripture in the Bible to comfort me. I need some answers, Lord. Please guide me."

As I began to open my Bible, I saw the angel that was taped on the inside cover. With tears, I remembered our old house. I remembered quality family time. With that angel and God's help, I opened my Bible directly to the beginning of the book of Job.

After reading the book of Job and calming myself with God's Word, I could see how little faith I had compared to Job. I still had my wife and daughters. I did not have sores covering my body. I still had my friends, and I had more blessings than I could ever count. Job lost it all but still did not turn away from God. He cursed the day he was born. He lashed out in anger, but he never turned his back on God. I had nothing on Job. God was saying to me, "So what now, Karl? Are you going to give up on me? Quit? Look what I did for you. I died on the cross for you and you're going to give up?"

I had to go down the mountain into the valley to gain momentum to make it up the next hill. I had to be humble and yield to the Lord just as Job had. There is sorrow in a loss, especially one so unexpected, but out of sorrow those tears water a new plant of faith and hope. Out of sorrow we grow stronger. Anyone can have faith in God when times are good; although often those are the times we feel we do not need Him. The ability to endure through difficult circumstances solidifies our foundation in Christ.

Around this time, I met a man named Harold Girvin. He was the father of my sister-in-law, and he had a special craft. He made angels out of metal coffee can lids. These angels were beautiful, intricate ornaments standing about three inches high. They had wings and robes, and held a small candle in one hand. A small Christmas tree ball formed the head. They could either be hung as an ornament or stand on their own. When my sister-in-law gave me one as a Christmas gift, it captivated me like the child's angel drawing on my mom's bedroom door. I was fascinated by Harold's creation and wanted to meet him.

Eventually, I was given the chance to meet Harold at his house. A humble and soft spoken man in his late 60s, he went over the process only once. I was eager to learn how to make these angels. He showed me all the tools I needed—needle-nose pliers, an awl, tin cutter, electrical wire for the candle and a small Christmas ball for the head—and gave me a pattern to start.

In fact, someone else had taught Harold how to make the angels. Harold tweaked the original design and in time, I changed it even more. No one seems to know the originator of the angels. I personally tried to find him, but was unsuccessful.

I started making the angels at my work bench in my garage, moving inside the house when it got too cold. The first ones weren't great, but soon my angels looked fairly nice. At first, I made them for our Christmas tree, but I began giving a few to special friends. It took time to make them—about 30 minutes for each angel. I had a feeling of ownership, and that made it harder to give them away. I wasn't sure who I would give angels to. I needed to listen to God.

As time passed, I began to realize I never really owned them. I had some more growing to do that would surprise even me. God was going to reveal to me my gift for talking to people on a personal level, one-on-one. He was going to show me I could affect the lives of other people that a few years earlier I would not have given a second glance. My angels were ready for my ministry, but God had a little more work to do in me.

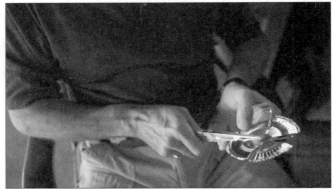

Mike and James

Again, I tell you that if two of you on earth agree about anything
you ask for, it will be done for you by my Father in heaven.
Matthew 18:19 (NIV)

 $\mathcal{T}$ he first time I saw Mike Couch, he was standing on his porch,
smoking a cigarette and drinking a cup of coffee. He was a single,
slender, 26-year-old man in old, green baggy pants and a blue University of Kentucky basketball hat. Shortly after my brother's death,
my family and I spent a week near Harlan, Kentucky to help repair
homes with fellow church members. The coordinator of the job site
warned us about Mike. Among his other infractions of the law, he
grew and sold marijuana, but God led me to volunteer myself, Barb,
six-year-old Angie and four-year-old Lindsey to help repair and paint
the outside of his house.

I walked up on the porch to introduce myself. I'm still not exactly
sure why I said what I did, except God gave me the words.

"So, you're the guy who grows marijuana," I said.

"How do you know that?" he asked, startled.

"It doesn't matter," I replied. "Don't worry, I'm not a cop, but I
don't think you should be doing what you're doing. Someday you'll
get busted, but I'm not going to turn you in. That's not what I'm
here for."

With those cards out on the table, we began to talk rather comfortably, much more so than I thought I would with a man who sold drugs. Throughout the first day, I talked to him about my mom and brother passing away and my acceptance of Jesus. I wanted to stress the urgency of knowing God's plan for each of us.

"You know, Mike," I said, "there's a Bible verse I love to quote, James 4:14: 'How do you know what will happen tomorrow? For your life is like the morning fog—it's here a little while, then it's gone.'" I told him you never know when the Lord is going to knock on your door, but you better be ready to open it.

The next morning and every morning thereafter, Mike looked worn-down from a night of dealing drugs, but there was a hunger in his eyes to know more about God. We spent a lot of time talking to each other over the next few days. In fact, many of the conversations were initiated by Mike. It was my first glimpse of how hungry people are for the word of God.

One day, Mike asked me to follow him into the woods. We sat down on a fallen tree next to some of his marijuana plants. I could almost see the devil sitting on one of his shoulders and an angel on the other. He wanted to look slick and in charge, but he wouldn't have asked me to come along if he didn't want to hear what I had to say.

After Mike made sure I knew what the plants were, he sat there fidgeting for a while, kicking stones and breaking sticks. Then he said, "Well, Karl, how do you know there is a God?"

"Well," I said, "what can we do to make you believe there is a God?"

After a little more fidgeting, he said, "You see the big tree over there? I want God to uproot it and put it down over there."

It was time for me to speak to the Lord. Silently, I prayed, "Lord, I do know the Bible says we can move trees, even move mountains, but you have to have a lot of faith. Lord, I don't have that kind of faith. Can you help Mike think of something we can do, so we can pray for it to happen and show him you're up there? Mike doubts you and needs you to prove that you are there. When I challenge you, my prayers are answered. I know you can do that for him."

I looked over at Mike and saw he had a stick in his hands. It was a small stick and it had one branch, about as thick as a pencil, sticking out of it. He stuck the stick in the ground like he was planting a flag and said, "OK, Karl, where the branch comes out, I want it to bend over and break. Then I'll know there's a God up there."

I looked up through the trees and whispered my thank you. Then I looked squarely at Mike and said, "We can do this, but you have to help me. In the Bible, Matthew 18:19-20, it says if two of you agree down on Earth concerning anything you ask for, God will provide it. It goes on to say where two or three gather together because they are mine I will be there among them. Mike, you can go first. You can pray silently, or out loud. I'll wait a few minutes, and then I'll pray."

Mike prayed silently, and then I prayed a short prayer out loud. When I finished, it was quiet and still in the woods. We both sat and stared at the stick like it was a mesmerizing campfire. As we sat and stared, I saw the branch begin to move. Call it the breath of God or the hand of an angel, the branch was bending, and it continued to bend. I wanted to shout. I wanted to jump up and down and scream to Mike, but I controlled myself. "Lord, let Mike be the one to say something to me, so I will know you are proving to him you are up there," I prayed silently.

Mike looked up at me, his eyes a little larger than they were a few minutes ago. "Did you see that, Karl? The stick bent!"

"I saw it, Mike. I'm telling you God is alive, and He wants you to sit up and take notice. He loves and cares for you. He doesn't want you growing marijuana and getting in trouble. He's trying to help you."

"But the branch didn't break," Mike said.

"It sure looked like it was going to, though, didn't it?"

"Yeah, but it didn't break."

I thought to myself, "Lord, maybe we need God to shake this man awake."

"You saw it, and I saw it," I said. "God is trying to tell you something here. I hope you can figure out how to hear it."

We walked back down to the house, and I finished up my work. As we were getting ready to leave, I said something to Mike about reading the Bible, and asked him if he had one. He answered that he did.

"Wouldn't it be amazing," I said, "if you read from the Bible tonight, and I came back tomorrow and told you where you read from."

"Yeah, right, Karl. Now that would be amazing. That would be a miracle if you could do that."

"It's not me, Mike, but if I pray about it, God will lead me to where you will read from tonight. He's going to show you He cares and loves you. Are you going to read tonight?"

"Yeah, I'll read tonight."

I went back to the barracks feeling exhilarated, invigorated and almost intoxicated. I shared the remarkable things that happened with the rest of the church group, and then I was alone with my Bible and the Lord. I was a little scared, and a little panicked. I wondered if I could pull this one off.

But then I prayed, and I knew I wasn't going to find it by myself. God would lead me to a chapter. I asked for guidance, and I opened my Bible to the beginning of a book, as I did when my brother had passed away.

This time it was the Book of James. I read the short book, and it touched me how much the book talked about what Mike and I had been discussing the other day, and how practical it was to his life. I thought this had to be it. It was short enough for Mike to read and seemed to be the perfect fit. I was excited, like a kid on Christmas Eve. I couldn't sleep.

As we drove up to Mike's house the next morning, I noticed he didn't look quite as worn and tired as he had on the other mornings. The first thing he told me was that he read his Bible.

"I read a whole book of the Bible," he said proudly.

"I bet I know where you read from," I said confidently, especially when he said he read an entire book.

"Yeah, right, Karl. You don't know where I read from."

"Mike, don't you remember I told you God would lead me to where you were reading to show you how much he cares for you?"

"Well then, Karl, where did I read from?"

"You read the book of James," I said.

His eyes were wider than they had been when the stick bent. His mouth dropped open, and he was speechless.

"You know, Mike, I'm nobody special, but God has performed miracles the past few days to show you He is here, there and everywhere. He cares about you. I think it's about time you did your part. God's speaking to you loud and clear that He loves you. Get your life straightened out. Become involved in a church. You've already tried the other side of life, and it isn't working out or you wouldn't be standing here talking to me. You're only headed for more trouble."

We were finished working at Mike's house, but I made arrangements to meet him Friday night before we headed home. He didn't think I would show up, but I surprised him.

On Friday, I drove to Mike's house. I prayed and hoped he would see God's light that night. As I pulled in the driveway, Mike was sitting on the porch. I walked up to him and gave him a hug.

"You know, Mike," I said, "we covered a lot of ground this week. I want to let you know I love you, and I accept you as you are. I used to smoke. I used to party. I could swear with the best of them, but God took those things from me one at a time. He'll do the same for you."

"Karl, you're really disappointed I didn't accept Jesus as my personal Savior this week."

"No Mike, I'm not disappointed. You can't do this for me. That's the wrong reason. You have to take Him into your heart. I can't do that for you. You can't do it to please me."

I'll never forget what he told me. "You know, Karl, if I accept Christ in my heart, you'll be the first to know."

It had been an emotional week for both of us. As I glanced down at his feet, for the first time I noticed Mike's worn and tattered shoes.

"Mike, you're not going to believe this, but God has one more miracle up his sleeve," I said. "Before we came on this trip, I bought a pair of work shoes. When I came home from the store I wore them a few days, and they just didn't feel right. As we were packing, I threw them in the trunk of my car, and prayed God would bring someone across my path that could fill those shoes. I forgot about them until this very moment. I want you to have them."

I went to the trunk, brought them out and he tried them on. They fit perfectly.

"Mike, God is something else, isn't He?" I said. "He even gave you a new pair of shoes. Don't ever forget what happened here this week. We shared a lot and God showed you He's up there, alive and well. All you have to do is open your eyes, and come to Him. That's the way God works. You can't do it for me. It's between you and God."

We exchanged addresses, and we wrote a lot of letters through the years. He sent me Bible verses and poems, and he even sent me a cross that had been very special to him. I sent him Christian music and money every once in a while. I also sent him one of my angels. After all, he was a special person in my life. There were a few years I didn't hear anything from him. Unfortunately, he was caught growing marijuana and was sent to prison.

Through Mike's letters, I knew he was studying the Bible and growing closer to God. Some of us have the opportunity to plant the seeds, some of us water the plants, and some harvest the crops. Mike was an important part in my spiritual life, and I was the same in his. He taught me to accept people as they are. We can't do the work for someone; we have to show them the tools and how to use them. God used Mike as a stepping stone for my ministry. God used this time to give me confidence in my ability to relate to people one on one.

How beautiful upon the mountains are the feet of those who bring the happy news of peace and salvation, the news that the God of Israel reigns.
Isaiah 52:7 (TLB)

III
Lifted Up By Angels

We're lifted up by angels
given wings to fly
leave the night behind us
trust the Light to find us
even as we rise.
We're lifted up by angels

Jennifer Kimball
Tom Kimmel

I think I know how Jonah felt. The Lord was giving me tools for my ministry. He sent me to Kentucky for preparation. Now, He was pointing to a new ministry—a ministry with the angels made from the lids of coffee cans. I was getting good at making them, and I was proud of how nice they looked. I gave them to people who were special to me, but the Lord wanted me to go one step further. These angels were to become the silent heralds, the centerpiece of my ministry. I felt God prodding me to make these angels, give them away to strangers and share Christ with them. For quite some time I struggled with what

God actually wanted me to do. God has the wrong guy, I thought. Jonah thought the same thing and he lost his way. God encouraged me one more time. "Remember, I died on the cross for you. I tasted the vinegar used to wet my lips. I did that for you. This is the least you can do for me."

It struck a cord deep inside me. I would make the angels and use them to share the Word of God. I would ask God to lead me to the people who wanted and needed what Christ could offer. This was my mission. I embraced the idea with both the fervor and fear of a young boy waiting for his first ride on a roller coaster. It was the beginning of a ride of a lifetime.

I prepared my angels and myself for when God would tap me on the shoulder and say, "This person needs an angel." The first opportunity came sooner than I expected, and the last one is not yet in sight. The following stories are small examples of how my ministry has grown and some of the blessings God has given me since my angels first took flight.

Junkyard Angels

So do not fear, for I am with you; not be dismayed,
for I am your God. I will strengthen you and help you;
I will uphold you with my victorious right hand.
Isaiah 41:10 (NIV)

In 1988, I needed a new fan for our Chevrolet Malibu. It had broken and dented the hood from underneath. I felt fortunate, because a few days earlier, I was leaning over the running engine performing a tune-up. Buying another fan didn't seem like such a big deal considering what could have happened if the blade had broken while I was hovering over it.

So I went to a local junkyard to get the fan part I needed. As I was waiting at the parts counter, a rough-looking man came walking in the store. He was covered with tattoos, jeans, leather and chains. Through his long, straggly beard, he bellowed, "I can't wait till the (expletive) bars open. I want to get (expletive) plastered." He went on his loud, brash way, making me increasingly uncomfortable. I wanted to get my part and get out of there. Then the Lord spoke to me, "This person, Karl."

"Excuse me Lord," I said, "but are you crazy? There is no way a guy like this is going to listen to me. I can't do this, Lord."

This unnerving man was swearing in one ear, and God was

whispering in the other. I got my fan part and left, feeling a little disappointed that I didn't talk to the man. I drove a short distance and pulled off to the side of the road and prayed, expressing my sorrow in letting God down. I couldn't do it. I was scared. I had a ton of work to do at home, and I had to fix my car. I promised myself if I ever ran into him again I would share Christ with him. I felt better. I squeezed out of that one, I thought, but it wasn't long until I discovered God makes us live up to our promises.

A few days later, the rearview mirror fell off the car. Guess which junkyard had the best price? God seemed to be reminding me of my promise. I wrapped one of my angels, knowing what God had in store for me. At the parts counter I bought my mirror, looked around a bit anxiously and asked whether the guy with the tattoos and beard came around often. I learned he came in regularly but hadn't been in today.

I sighed with relief, but I felt somewhat disheartened. Maybe I was reading too much into God's leads. I had the angel wrapped and ready to go, so I gave it to the man at the parts counter, and I thanked him for all of his help.

"Hey, I've got something for you, too," he responded, giving me a company calendar and pen.

With mirror, calendar and pen in hand, I left the building feeling more disappointed. "Lord, I thought for sure he would be here," I said in a silent prayer. "I don't understand. I thought this is what you wanted. What are you trying to do, Lord, make a fool out of me?"

I took a few more steps to my car, and suddenly there he was, tattoos and all, walking toward me. As we passed, I turned to speak to him but no words came out of my mouth. He brushed by, stopped and turned to me.

"Hey buddy, you got something you want to say to me?" he asked harshly.

"Yeah, as a matter of fact I do," I said, my spiritual strength returning with my speech. "You know, I was here last week, and all you could talk about was going to the bars and getting drunk. That's really cool. The morning after is really cool, too, when you have your face stuck down in the toilet, your head feels like it's been hit with a hammer, and your stomach is spinning like a merry-go-round. That's no life to lead, and you're not happy with it either. I don't know if you go to church, but I'd like to share Christ with you."

His eyes welled up with tears.

"You don't know me," I continued, "and I don't know you, but whether you believe it or not God set up our meeting. The life you're leading isn't what God wants from you, and it isn't what you want either."

He looked at me and said, "You know, my dad's a pastor."

Without thinking, I said, "I'm sorry."

We both chuckled at that comment because we all know pastor's kids have extra pressures. Rebellion is not uncommon. I told him I had a gift for him, but I gave it to the clerk inside. With my new pen, I wrote his phone number on the calendar, and told him I'd call to make arrangements to deliver my handcrafted gift to him.

A week later the angel was ready, and I called to ask where he lived. He lived in front of the junkyard. I didn't remember seeing a house when I was there the first two times. When I arrived at the junkyard, I saw the house fit in with the junkyard decor. Walking to the door, two barking dogs made me a bit nervous. When I discovered no one was home, I placed the angel on an old barbecue grill on the porch and let the dogs have their territory.

I knew I planted the seed God wanted me to plant. I was obedient in sharing Christ. It wasn't easy—in fact it was frightening—but the gratifying feeling of knowing I did what God wanted me to do gave me the power and the courage to continue with my angel ministry.

An angel had flown out of my control, and it wasn't as hard to let it go as I thought it would be. God was making the angels fly, and He was using me to place the angels where He wanted them to go.

Angels in the Mall

He was alone at the time as his disciples had
gone into the village to buy some food.
John 4:8 (TLB)

$\mathcal{I}$ was not a coffee drinker, so I had to scrounge for coffee can lids to make the angels. Friends, family, fellow church members and co-workers kept me supplied. I had the lids and the tools, but as I was making the angels, I wondered who God planned to receive them. Where would I meet these people? God led me to the answer through prayer, and the Spirit told me to go where there are many people. Where are all the people? They are at the mall. Park City Center, a large local mall, is a hub of activity, especially around the holidays. In December 1988, I started giving my angels to strangers at the mall at Christmastime.

I wrapped the angels in Christmas wrapping paper, but I felt I should add something else. God led me to include a Bible verse, Matthew 5:14-16: "The angel I made you is a reminder God is with you through good times and bad times. The candle represents that you are the light of the world. Keep letting your light shine for all to be seen. May God bless you."

I folded a paper with these words and tucked it in with each angel as I wrapped them.

I had been to the mall many times, but as I entered this time, I was more attentive to the hustle and bustle. I found a bench, sat down, and prayed, "I don't know who you want me to give these gifts to, Lord, but I want you to lead the right people to me."

People with bright shopping bags were heading in every direction. Christmas carols filled the air, adding extra excitement to my anxiety and apprehension. I sat with my angels in a large plastic bag waiting for God to give me some direction, and I wondered how long Noah had to sit with a boat in his backyard waiting for rain while his neighbors laughed at him.

Then God spoke to me and told me to give the angels to people in wheelchairs. That seemed easy enough until I started looking around. There must have been wheelchair races at the mall. Wheelchairs zoomed to my left and right, and I only had so many angels in my bag. God likes to test me with his sense of humor. Finally I felt God leading me to give an angel to a person in a wheelchair that I saw twice. I waited to see someone in a wheelchair I had seen before. More than an hour later, I finally saw a young woman for the second time. I wondered what her disability was, and I felt good offering her an angel. God had some lessons planned for me this night.

I approached her and said, "You are a very special person. God wants me to give this gift to a person in a wheelchair that I have seen twice tonight, and you're the one."

She replied, "Why would you give me a gift? I don't want a gift from you."

I was embarrassed and felt like running to the nearest exit.

"Please take this gift," I said. "God wants you to have this gift because you are a special person."

"Thank you," she said, "but I still don't understand why you're giving me a gift."

I gave her the gift and headed for the exit with the other angels undistributed. I wanted out of there like a kid trapped in school on a bright, sunny day. I mumbled to God, I didn't understand why he would lead me here to make me feel so worthless. She didn't even want the gift.

As I walked on, grumbling and feeling sorry for myself, I had a sensation I never felt before or since. My feet tingled, and they weren't touching the ground. For 10 feet or so, I was lifted into the air, and then gently dropped back down. It was an overwhelming feeling. I prayed, "Lord that was incredible what you did back there. I'm sorry, and I'll stay. Forgive me for not having enough faith. I'll go back and hand out the rest of my angels. I love you, Lord."

I went back to the center of the mall and began handing out the rest of the gifts to people who came into my view for a second time. No one said "thank you" or "Hallelujah" or "praise the Lord." It wasn't quite what I expected.

Later that evening, sitting at home, I asked Barb if I was really cut out for this. I felt like a balloon that had lost its air, limp and useless. I heard the phone ring. Barb answered it, and then handed me the phone.

"Are you Karl Miller?" a man on the other end asked. "Are you the one who was giving out angels at the mall today?"

"Yes, that's me," I said.

"You gave me an angel today and I was so excited someone would do that for me I had to find you and thank you. You signed your name on the piece of paper that was with the angel, and when I looked in the phone book there was only one Karl with a 'K.' What organization do you belong to?"

"Organization?" I asked. "I'm not part of any organization. It's only me and God."

"I can't believe someone would do this for people they don't know" the man continued. "I want to encourage you to keep doing what you're doing. It really lifted me up. It is a wonderful ministry."

As I thanked him and hung up the phone, I also thanked God for the encouragement I needed to continue my ministry. I thanked God for the mustard seed of faith that had been planted within me. I needed to learn how to follow God and allow Him to lead me.

My first course, Angels 101, was over, and I passed. Did God make a mistake with the first woman in the wheelchair because she was not appreciative? No, God has a way of keeping us in our place. God didn't want me to expect a miracle every time I handed out an angel, but then God turned right around and gave me the encouragement I needed with the phone call. I continued my ministry at the mall every year, no matter what was happening in my life, as long as God called me to do it.

I was self-conscious about my ministry at first. I didn't want to be a scripture-spouting evangelist who turned people off. It had to be a more subtle ministry that included everyday conversation. The Lord had already provided me with many life stories I was able to share. I wanted people to know how my life had changed, and how much more fulfilled their life could be with the guidance of God.

I began to make a few more angels every year. God gave me several different ways to approach people or for them to approach me. A sure sign, stemming back to the days of the stolen watch and the watch my mom gave me, was for someone to ask me the time. I knew right away God wanted them to receive an angel. Often, I would sit on a bench and wait for the next person to be guided my way. Conversations started easily with the weather and eventually I knew when to give them a gift and when to ask them about their spiritual life. I encouraged people to start their walk with the Lord by finding a church.

Not every angel gift provided a great story, but there were enough encouraging conversations to keep my head up every year. But every once in a while, God would throw me a curveball.

Eyes and Ears

But those that hope in the Lord will renew their strength.
They will soar on wings like eagles; they will run and
not grow weary, they will walk and not be faint.
Isaiah 40:31 (NIV)

Each Christmas was a little different. One year, God called me to stand in the center of the mall and give my angels to people who looked less fortunate than others. I gave the angels to people who looked like a trip to the mall was a tense, struggling experience for them because there wasn't enough money to get the gifts they really wanted. I would share God with these people and hope the angels would lift their spirits.

With my last few angels in hand, a young, blonde girl in her late teens came up to me and pointed to my watch. I gave her the time, and then said to her, "You're a very special person. God led you here, and I'm supposed to give you this gift."

I shared more with her and told her about Christ's love. As she was about to turn and go, she said, "Thank you very much."

I talked to her for quite some time. I didn't realize she was deaf. I wouldn't have picked her out in a crowd as someone who needed an angel. God, once again, was opening my eyes to see that no matter what people look like, rich or poor, pretty or plain; we are all in need of His grace, mercy and love.

I was high on this realization, feeling good about handing out another angel, when I felt a tap on my shoulder. "Hey buddy," the older man who tapped me said, "my wife and I have been watching you for about an hour now, and we noticed you are handing out gifts to people as they walk by. Are you part of an organization?"

I explained to them how I started making the angels after my mom passed away and how it turned into my own personal ministry.

"Well, can you tell us one thing?" the man continued. "Why did you give an angel to that young girl? She didn't seem to fit in with the rest of the people you were giving gifts to."

I shared the story of the watch and said, "I gave her a gift because she asked me what time it was and that was how I knew God wanted her to have an angel. And do you know what? She was deaf. I would have never picked her to receive an angel, but the Lord sent her my way. It's amazing how God works."

We talked for a while, and I told them I had been nominated to be an elder in my church, but I had a few reservations. Although I read my Bible, at times I did not feel like I knew enough to fill the position of an elder. I still felt God calling me to get more involved in my church.

The man looked at me and said, "Son, watching you do what you're doing tonight, your church will be lucky to have you as an elder. By the way, I'm an elder in my church, and I have no doubts you will do a wonderful job."

I was amazed how God used this man to encourage me. I handed him and his wife an angel.

"No," he said, "save your angels for someone else."

"Please take it," I said. "You were the eyes of God watching me tonight, and I know God wants you to have this. Isn't God something the way He works?"

"Yeah, you're something else, too," he said with a smile as they walked away.

It had never occurred to me I was being watched at the mall. I guess I should have at least suspected security cameras, but it made me realize no matter where we are—at the mall, at work, at the beach, or all alone in the middle of a forest—we are being watched by the eyes of God. He is always watching; ready to pick us up when we fall, to weep when we grieve, and to rejoice in our happiness.

The next year, I was back at the mall, sitting on a bench with my angels beside me. A man sat down, and we began talking about work and the possibility of layoffs at both of our places of employment.

His wife came along, and as they were getting ready to leave, I said, "I have a little something for you. I'd like you to have this gift. I was praying the next person who sat beside me would get this, and you are the one."

I went on to explain why I was making these gifts and how my life had changed. Trying not to ramble too much, I told them about the events surrounding my mom's funeral. One of my worst fears is overwhelming people with too many stories, but this couple seemed very interested. They showed no signs of wanting to leave, although I kept asking them if I was getting too long-winded. I invited them to get involved in a church and if they did not have one I assured them they would be welcome at my church.

They asked a few more questions, and finally I said, "If I tell you any more stories, you'll know what the gift is before you unwrap it."

The woman sitting there said, "Oh, I already know what's in here. You gave an angel to my daughter last year. She has blonde hair and she is deaf, if you happen to remember her."

I was speechless. She went on to say the angel was an answered prayer for them. Before that December day one year ago, their daughter had become rebellious and had been hanging out with the wrong crowd.

The girl's mother stared at me and smiled.

"We're not sure why, but after you gave her that angel her life turned around," she said. "Her defiance stopped and she got involved in a church. It was like a miracle."

I told them exactly what happened the night I met their daughter. Sitting on the hard benches at the mall, with commotion all around, I felt like I was in my living room talking to old friends. It felt so good I had made a difference. I often don't get to see or hear about the fruits of my ministry. Of all the angels I have given out, there are only a handful of people I get to talk to again.

Then the light bulb went off in my head. I had a purpose in all of this, but so did their daughter. It was not the daughter that needed the help anymore.

"Do you think the Lord is trying to tell you something here?" I said. "This is quite a coincidence for me to sit down, almost exactly one year later, next to the parents of someone who I gave an angel to. What are the chances of this happening? Your daughter got the message, but did you? Please listen to God because He is trying to touch your heart. Read the Bible. Pray. Find a church in which you are comfortable. God is encouraging you. This is no coincidence. This is a miracle."

They thanked me again and walked away with their angel. They had been moved and encouraged to grow deeper in their relationship with God. It was almost like the way I felt when my mom was still alive. I felt I didn't have to worry about prayer because she was always praying for me. They had their daughter back, and weren't concentrating on their spiritual lives. Apparently God wanted them to grow more on their spiritual walk with Him.

Not all of my encounters at the mall were quite so dramatic, but through the years I managed to have some very interesting conversations with many different types of people. It became increasingly easier to start conversations and to share my life stories. I began to realize that so many of us long for spiritual contact, but for some reason it's taboo to talk about it in a public place. Once people realized I was not going to preach to them, they would open up.

Through these experiences, I had the chance to interact with a wide variety of people. I became a marriage counselor for a couple in their eighties. I spoke with mechanics, executives, brides-to-be, children and grandmothers. They all received angels. Often I would start a conversation by asking about a person's church Christmas program.

I once used this method with a person who was Moravian. Now, I hadn't seen a Moravian Christmas service, but after listening to this man for nearly 20 minutes, I could hear the children's choir and taste the hot coffee and sugar cakes as if I had been there. He was as excited as a child watching fireworks. His eyes shone as brightly as the candles he described.

Often, my conversations would lead to discussions of various church denominations. I met people who had been turned off by a certain church and never bothered to look for another one. I always tell people we all partake in different ceremonies, attend different services and say different words, but we are all equal in God's eyes. I urged many people to find a church that suited them and not to take the easy way out by saying they tried church once, but it didn't work for them.

I was even surprised one evening at the mall to find myself seated beside a pastor, telling him my stories. I realized even pastors need to hear encouragement. We shared the trials and tribulations of witnessing to people and trying to make it meaningful.

One of the most uplifting encounters I had was with a young boy who had braces on both his legs. He sat down beside me with a large smile and immediately asked what was in my bag. Clearly this was a sign from God. It wasn't his disability that made him special, it was his smile. This boy was not only enduring difficulty in his life, but he also was enjoying every moment. It was evident his presence helped his family enjoy life more, too. He thought I was Santa Claus and he loved his angel, but his smile will continue to be his gift to me for years to come.

There have been countless conversations over the years, some emotional and striking, some mundane and ordinary. But all of them have been important to me and to God. I can only hope and pray I can continue to touch and be touched by the wings of my angels.

Ice Angel

No eye has seen, no ear has heard, no mind has conceived
what God has prepared for those who love him.
1 Corinthians 2:9 (NIV)

One Saturday evening, after I had been sharing my angels at the mall, I was eagerly anticipating an annual Christmas party at the home of a good friend. The day had been particularly exhilarating, but mentally tiring. The two seemed to go hand in hand, like working on a car engine all day long and getting it to hum, but then wanting to rest and feel good about what was accomplished. I could already feel the warmth of my friend's cozy basement where we always met.

Once we got to the party, relaxing in the glow of friendship, we shared the highlights of the past few weeks. We ate, sang carols and waited for Santa Claus to saunter down the steps. Our hostess took the annual photos of Santa handing out gifts to all the children and adults, and then she told us her nephew carved ice sculptures. He was going to create one for us that night, and anyone that wanted to watch was welcome to come outside.

"No thanks," I thought. That would mean putting on my coat and standing around in the cold, watching a guy with a chain saw hack away at a block of ice. I was warm and toasty, and I decided to stay in the basement with a few other friends who didn't want to go out in the cold. Curiosity got the best of my family, and they decided to go up and take a look at the ice sculpture. A few minutes later Barb came back down.

"Karl," she said, "you have to come out and see what he is creating. It is amazing."

Toasty or not, I decided to go see what he was carving. Out in the cold, I was struck by the blue and purple lights shining behind the block of ice. Slowly, my eyes focused on the ice itself. He was carving an angel. Standing there in the chilly night air, I felt the warmest I had all evening. He would lop off an imperfection of the ice with the chain saw and then use another tool to refine the figure. With the sculptor's great dexterity and care, the angel took form, and lifted my spirit high into the winter sky. The lights melted the outer layers, making them smooth and translucent, almost transparent. I knew the angel was for me. I had been a faithful servant that day, and God wanted to warm me. So what does He do? He takes me into the cold night air to be enriched and nourished, and I almost missed this encounter with God. I stood there and cried, feeling wealthier than a millionaire.

As I watched the artist carve away the imperfections in the ice, it struck me that God does the same thing with every one of us. He chips away one imperfection and smoothes it, and repeats the process. Like that angel, we are transparent to God. He sees straight through to our hearts. He knows all of our imperfections. He knows when we are putting on masks and trying to be someone we're not, but He still cares enough for us to keep chipping away.

As the sculptor finished, a perfect angel was left standing for us to admire, but God's work with us never stops. He never puts down his tools. He is continually chipping away at us, molding and forming us in his likeness.

Whoever said Cleanliness
is Next to Godliness?

Houses and wealth are inherited from parents,
but a prudent wife is from the Lord.
Proverbs 19:14 (NIV)

God keeps us on our toes. As soon as we think we have everything in a neat little package, God shows us our box is not big enough to contain Him.

One Sunday night, I wanted to put on my robe and sit down with the Sunday paper to relax. With work during the week and sharing my angels on Saturday, this Sunday evening was mine to relax. As I opened the paper, the doorbell rang. Barb answered it, and came into the living room where I was sitting.

"Karl," she said, "there's a young woman at the door who is really upset. She needs help with her car. She has a flat tire, and was too scared to stop the car on the highway at night."

We live near an exit of an interstate highway, but why our house? Why this Sunday night?

"Can't she use our phone and call someone to come get her?" I said without looking up from the paper. Barb didn't respond immediately, but from her silence, I got the feeling she didn't like my answer.

"Karl, I don't believe you!" she exclaimed. "You were out at the mall trying to encourage people this weekend, and now someone stops by our house, crying and upset, and you don't even want to help."

Embarrassed and ashamed, I put on my old work clothes and went to see what I could do. I can fix almost anything that has an engine and wheels, and this was only a flat tire, so in a short time I could be back in my robe, reading the paper. She drove a beat up old Ford with an old tire on it. She had driven several miles on a flat, so the tire was somewhat shredded. She was lucky to have made it to our house.

I climbed into the driver's seat. The inside of the car looked like a trash can from a convenience store. Wrappers, milk cartons, potato chip bags, soda cans and debris littered the tattered interior. I'm a very neat person. I like everything orderly and in its place. Looking at this car sent shudders of disgust up and down my spine. As I was driving it up the driveway to the garage, I felt like I was on an amusement park ride, bouncing up and down to the rhythm of a shredded tire.

Luckily, the lady had a spare, because the flat tire could not be fixed. I put air in the spare tire and used my floor jack to raise the car. I changed the tire quickly, but then I noticed her doors squeaked when they opened and closed. A few shots of WD-40 later, the doors were working better than anything else on the car. She appreciated my extra effort, and thanked me repeatedly for my help.

As she got into her car to leave, she said, "You know, I was praying the Lord would lead me to someone who could fix my tire. I didn't know which way to turn, but I ended at your house. You answered my prayer."

Those words crashed down like thunder. Sure, I wanted to rest, but when God wants to use us, we'd better be ready. I felt humbled, which wasn't the first time, and it certainly wouldn't be the last. This woman put her faith in God, and I was almost too blind to see anything more than empty milk cartons and bare seat springs. God loves her every bit as much as He loves me, and I prayed I could be more attuned to what God had in store for me.

For the Angel of the Lord guards and rescues all who reverence him.
Psalms 34:7 (TLB)

Angels, God and Pizza

Those of steadfast mind you keep in peace–
in peace because they trust in you.
Isaiah 26:3 (NRSV)

One December day in 1993, I took my lunch break at a local pizza shop. I work at a company with thousands of employees, and it seemed like all of them, plus the rest of the city, wanted pizza that day. After ordering my food, I was unable to find an open table. Back in the corner, my eye caught an empty chair at a table for two. A man was eating alone, so I asked if I could join him. He said he'd be glad for the company, so I sat down, bowed my head and said a short prayer. We recognized each other, and after some brief introductions, we soon realized we worked at the same company, but in different areas. I told Jim I worked in the advertising department.

"Hey," Jim said, "I heard they are going to sell the advertising division and move you guys back to the manufacturing plant. Does that bother you?"

Did that bother me? Jim didn't know how I felt. I had found out a few days earlier about the sale of the advertising division. I was going from a prominent daytime job back to shift work at the factory, not to mention taking a pay cut. I was more than bothered by it. I was consumed by fear and doubt about my future.

"Yes, it does bother me," I said. "I have been in advertising for 18 years, and this will be a big change for me, but I know God doesn't make mistakes."

The last thing I said was mostly rhetoric, because I honestly wasn't sure God knew what He was doing. I was feeling depressed, and my ego had taken a direct hit. We talked a little longer when, completely out of the blue, Jim said, "Hey, do you know angels are real?"

"What?" I answered, dumfounded.

"Do you know angels are real?" he repeated. "If you have the time, I have a story I'd like to tell you about how an angel helped us."

"I'd love to hear your story," I said. I was completely amazed how God was working. I found the only available seat in the restaurant, and I sat down, feeling discouraged, next to a guy who wanted to talk to me about angels. When we need a lift, God provides it. The following is Jim's story:

Several years before, Jim, his wife and their small baby were visiting friends when a snowstorm started. They thought they should go home, but before they realized it, the conversation with their friends kept them there another hour. The snow intensified, so their friends asked them to stay the night, but instead they decided to try and make it home.

They drove a few miles as the wind blew the near-blinding snow in horizontal sheets across their path. Still several miles from their house, they were making headway until they found themselves in a traffic jam with everyone else trying to reach their homes. They could see the flashing lights of a police car. Apparently, up ahead, there had been an accident.

Their baby started crying. They didn't have milk for the child and they were trapped in the traffic jam. There was an unspoken panic in the car when Jim remembered he had forgotten to fill the car with gas, and realized they must be running on fumes.

The only thing they could do was pray. They calmed themselves with a prayer asking God to send angels to get them out of this situation. Jim thanked God and they put their trust in Him. Shortly after they finished the prayer, they looked up and saw a man in a bright orange outfit with a matching hat looking in the windows of several cars ahead of them in the traffic jam. He would look in the windows, and then move on to the next car. The man in orange kept working his way back the line of cars in this blinding snowstorm. Jim and his wife wondered what this man was doing. When the man in orange got to their car, he motioned for them to roll the window down.

"I understand you're having some car trouble here and you're almost out of gas," the man in orange said.

"Yes, we are," Jim replied, astounded and wondering how he knew.

The man in orange continued, "In a few minutes, an ambulance is going to come by here. When the cars pull off the road to let the ambulance pass, I want you to pull in back of the ambulance and follow it. You will get home safely if you do as I say."

Dazed and a little confused, Jim rolled his window back up, but then his wife told him he forgot to thank the man. Jim quickly rolled the window down, but there was no one there. It was snowing hard, but this man's bright outfit should have been visible for the short distance he could have walked. Jim and his wife looked at each other in amazement, wondering what happened, but then they heard the siren from an ambulance. Everyone pulled off to the side of the road, and the couple did what the man in orange had told them to do. They pulled behind the ambulance and were able to pass cars stuck in the snow and the accident with no problems. They arrived at their house and opened the garage door, and as they pulled the car in the garage, it stalled and shut off. It was out of gas. Jim and his wife cried and thanked the Lord for getting them home safely.

After telling me this story and wiping some pizza from his chin, Jim asked me, "Do you believe in angels?"

"Yes I do. You're not going to believe this," I said. "I have never seen an angel, but I make angels." I told him I had been making angels for quite some time, and I shared my ministry with him.

"You know," I continued, "God is really amazing. I made a promise to God that I would hand out my angels every year at the mall, but this year I was feeling disheartened about my job. I wasn't going to go. So what does God do? He gives me one seat in this little pizza shop next to a man who has seen an angel. Jim, you have made my day. I wasn't sure if I had the strength and courage to go to the mall this year, but after hearing your story, I know I have to go. Thank you for being God's encouragement to me."

We shook hands and went back to work. God had, again, showed me He was there, ready to walk with me, no matter what. I had to put my own two feet on the ground and start moving.

What the Blind Boy Saw

But the fruit of the Spirit is love, joy, peace, patience,
kindness, goodness, faithfulness, gentleness and self-control.
Galatians 5:22-23 (NIV)

*N*ot everyone loses their job right before Christmas. Not everyone is forced to take a step back in their work. Listening to Jim's story about the angel was responsible for getting me back at the mall to witness that year. God gave me another sign earlier that year which should have given me a clue He was watching over me. My coffee can lid supply had been nearly exhausted. Because of my job situation, I wasn't searching for lids like I did other years. One day I walked down my driveway to get the mail. I found my mailbox was stuffed with a paper bag full of coffee can lids. To this day, I don't know who put them in my mailbox, but I know why they were put there.

As I sat on a bench at the mall, I prayed to myself. I told the Lord I felt like a hypocrite this year. I acknowledged His presence and my love for Him, but I didn't feel good about being there. As usual, I asked for guidance and that He would send a special person my way. I felt empty, and I wanted His love to shine through me despite my mood.

As I looked up after my prayer, I saw a family heading straight toward me—a man, a woman and their two sons. "Go sit next to the man on the bench," the father said to the younger son, as his mother led him over next to me.

I had never had such a quick response to a prayer. The mother and one of her sons sat down, and the boy kept creeping closer to me. His legs crowded me, and I thought, "Oh great. I don't even want to be here, and now this boy is practically sitting on my lap." The boy moved closer to me as the father and other son went off shopping.

A promise is a promise. I did not know how I was going to share my angel with this boy, but I knew I had to. I grabbed one of my wrapped angels out of my bag and said to the boy, "You are a very special person. I prayed whoever sat down next to me would get a gift, and you are the first person to sit here. I'd like you to have this gift."

As I handed him the package he fumbled with it and almost dropped it, as if he didn't really want it. I proceeded to tell this young boy I was handing out gifts because God asked me to try to touch people's hearts. I told him about the events surrounding my mom's death, and how I came to know God. I told him several other stories from my life. I was sure God was giving me the right words to say to this boy, but I still wasn't sure I wanted to be at the mall witnessing to people.

Finally, I said to him, "I don't know if you have ever had the opportunity to pray or have any prayers answered."

Then his mother spoke up. "Prayers? My son prays every day."

"He does?" I asked, thinking this boy hadn't even said a word to me. He kept pushing closer to my side, making me more uncomfortable.

"Sir," she said, "I don't know if you noticed, but my son is blind."

I was speechless.

"I didn't think you noticed," the mother said. "You know what my son prays for? He prays Jesus will come back so he can have his eyesight back."

God has a way of removing our self-pity. How could I not have noticed this boy was blind? I was so attuned to my own problems and frustrations I did not even notice he was blind. God was screaming in my ear, "Wake up Karl!"

As I sat there humbled, half ashamed and half revived, the father and other son came back to the bench. The father walked up to me and the first words out of his mouth were, "Hey buddy, do you know angels are real?"

"What?" I said, stunned.

"Do you know angels are real?" he said again, and he started telling me stories about angels. My mind was churning, and my soul was so dazzled I could not remember a word he said.

In the meantime, the son who had returned with the father began to help unwrap the gift I had given to the blind boy. "Dad, Dad," the boy said, tugging on his father's pants, "he makes angels. Look at this."

The father stopped his story, and we both looked at each other and shook our heads, smiling, not knowing what to say or exactly what happened. We all knew who created this moment.

The blind boy turned to me and said, "You know, I was really tired, and I had to sit down here beside you," he said.

"Son, you were meant to sit down here," I said. "God wanted you to have this angel. You are a very special person. God loves you very much."

"But I'm not tired anymore," the boy said. "I feel like I could run up and down the mall."

He got up and started shuffling and then running down the corridor. My first thought was, "Did he get his eyesight back?" His family ran after and caught up to him. He still couldn't see, but my eyes were opened. One of the most unforgettable images of my life is when the family turned to me, almost in unison, smiled and waved goodbye. I sat there and cried. A blind boy ministered to me.

No sooner had my eyes dried from that experience when a young woman came up to me and said, "Sir, could you tell me what time it is?" That question has always been God's cue to me to give them an angel.

I greeted her as I normally did, telling her God wanted me to give this gift to anyone who asked for the time. I handed her the wrapped package. "God loves you very much," I concluded.

"Thank you," she said, and left.

I was still trying to understand what happened with the blind boy, and I wished I could remember the angel stories the father had told me. Ten minutes later, the young woman came back to me and got down on her knees beside me.

"Sir," she said, "I had to come back and share this with you. You're my angel."

I thought to myself, "If she only knew what I felt like earlier today. I'm no angel."

She continued, "My best friend died this past week. I'm a Christian, but I cried out to God. I was angry with Him. I was really frustrated, and I wanted to know if He really cared about me anymore. I asked the Lord if He loves me, and if so, why did He take my best friend? My friend was a good person. She was healthy and too young to die. I didn't understand. I prayed God would send me a sign and let me know I was still loved, and you gave me a gift, this angel."

"You have no idea how much I needed to hear that story right now," I said. "Thank you for coming back and sharing with me."

"No, thank you," she said. "You're my angel, and you made my day."

She left me alone with my goose bumps. I knew what God was trying to tell me. Within a span of a few minutes, He took my empty cup and filled it until it was overflowing. He showed me it is OK to have an empty cup. God will not let us go because we lapse into self-pity, anger or even hatred. He will use someone else to nourish us and feed our spirit. God used those people to lift me higher than I had been in a long time. I felt like I could have flown out of the mall. We cannot do it on our own. God is ready, willing and waiting for us to call out to Him.

A Tale of Two Co-Workers

All of us must die eventually; our lives are like water that is
poured out on the ground—it can't be gathered up again.
But God will bless you with a longer life if you will
find a way to bring your son back from his exile.
2 Samuel 14:14 (TLB)

A co-worker of mine was 38 years old when our company re-organized, and he lost his job. We had worked together for many years, and in a blink he was gone. He was so young. I do not know what other factors were affecting him besides the loss of his job, but this co-worker turned to the bottle. Alcohol became his reason for living—and for dying. He spiraled downward like a plane with one wing. Food was irrelevant to him as long as he could get a drink. Eventually, he ended up in the hospital. He seemed determined on drinking himself to death.

The Lord spoke to me, urging me to go to this co-worker and talk to him. Over and over, I could feel the Lord tapping me on the shoulder and pointing the direction to take, but his wife kept telling me nothing could be done to make a difference. This man didn't care about me, about her, about their children or about God. He didn't want to see anyone, so I never visited him. I didn't want to step on anyone's toes. He died a sad and lonely death, and I have regretted my decision not to share Christ with him ever since. I often wonder if he ever made things right with God.

A year or so after his death, still feeling remorse, I made angels for his wife and children. I shared my spiritual life story with them, and I told his wife again I should have come to visit her husband. She reiterated it would not have made a difference, but I disagreed. God had spoken to me, and I felt ashamed I had ignored Him. I had made a big mistake, but I made a promise to God if there was ever an opportunity to help or guide a co-worker in a time of need, I would do it.

A year later, we got a phone call at work. A retired co-worker, Tom, was in the hospital. He had cancer and he was wondering why no one from work had come to see him. We heard he was not well and was in the hospital. Out of sight, out of mind has some validity in the daily grind, and none of us had been really close to him. Tom called to ask if someone, anyone, could come and visit him that evening in the hospital. No one offered. No one had the time, including me. It was Thursday, and I had to take my car to the shop after work. It would be late, but I would go. After all, I had promised God, and I could not let Him down again.

We worked late that evening. By the time I dropped my car off at the garage, arranged for a loaner and arrived at the hospital it was well past visiting hours. Maybe I looked official, but no one questioned why I was there so late. Again, I checked the room number on the paper that was crumpled in my pocket, and then I glanced in at Tom. I had to look twice at the sleeping figure to make sure it was him. I was taken aback by his frailty. His white skin hung over his bones like a wrinkled sheet. His cheeks were sunken and his eyes were yellow. One toe was left uncovered by his blanket.

"Lord," I prayed, "He's sleeping. I'll go in to him and touch his toe. If Tom wakes up, I'll talk to him and share Christ with him. If he doesn't, I'm out of here."

I moved to his bed and lightly touched his toe. Tom sat up like there were springs in his back. Startled, I jumped back two feet.

"I thought you were sleeping," I said. "I didn't expect you to wake up so fast."

Squinting and staring at me, Tom finally said, "Who are you?"

"Who am I?" I replied. "You called in to work asking us to come and see you, and you don't even know who I am?"

Tom focused a bit and looked at me. "Karl?" he asked.

"Yeah, that's right. I told you I'd make it in tonight," I said. "How are you feeling?"

He told me he had a little pain but it wasn't too bad. From all the tubes running in and out of his body, I knew he was probably on strong pain medication.

"I want to tell you why I'm here," I said. "We've talked a number of times about God before you retired, and I gave you one of my angels, but I was never sure if you accepted Christ as your personal Lord and Savior. I don't need to know. You know whether you have or not, but God has laid it on my heart to come here tonight and share Christ with you, and to pray with you. I'll be honest with you, that's why I'm here."

This wasn't how I normally witnessed to people. Usually, I'm not that blunt. I often find a way to weave my stories into a typical conversation, but I felt an urgency here that called for candor. We reminisced about work, and we shared updates about our families. I then asked if I could pray with him, and he agreed.

I prayed, "Lord, Thank you for this opportunity to come in here and share with Tom. I don't know if he's a Christian or not, but you do. If Tom hasn't found you, please keep him awake, all night if need be, to accept you as his personal Lord and Savior. Keep him awake until he surrenders to you. It was your direction that brought me here to be with him tonight and to pray for him. You led me here and I ask you now to guide and direct Tom. Make him part of your kingdom this very night. I ask all this in Jesus' name. Amen."

As I finished praying, I noticed Tom's eyes brightened through a thin film of tears. He shook my hand before I left and said, "Karl, I didn't think you would come. I didn't think anybody cared about me. Thanks for coming in here tonight. I really appreciate it."

I replied, "The Lord wanted me to come tonight. Think about it. Here it is, after 10 o'clock. It is after visiting hours, but no one has come in this room and asked me to leave. We serve an awesome God, and I really hope you consider what I shared with you tonight. I'm not here to judge you. You can fool me, but God knows your heart. It's getting serious for you now."

"Karl," he said, "will you come in again to see me? I really appreciate the time you spent here."

"Sure, I'll come in again."

"No, you won't be in again, Karl."

"Yes, I'll come in again," I promised. "I came in this time, didn't I? Remember, God sent me."

I left him with those last words. I went home that night feeling exhausted and relieved, like I had just played game seven of the World Series. Win or lose, I was playing. There are few things more tiring or fulfilling than being one of God's tools. Tom weighed heavily on me that weekend, and I was planning to go back to see him on Monday.

On Sunday, Barb picked up the newspaper and started paging through it.

"What was your co-worker's name you went to see on Thursday night?" she asked me.

I told her his name was Tom and asked her why she wanted to know, not realizing she was reading the obituaries.

"He died," she said.

I could hardly believe it. "What?" I said. "He did? When did he die?"

"The paper says he died Friday."

I was astounded. God gave me the opportunity to share, and God gave Tom the opportunity to set things straight with Him. Then God took Tom home. What a way to go. It gave me goose bumps. The timing was impeccable. Finally, I listened to what God was saying to me. I could have easily ignored God's calling. I was as busy as everyone else at work that night, but I kept my promise, and because of that I got to feel redemption from the failure I had felt with my other co-worker.

As I stood in front of the casket at Tom's viewing, I cried tears of joy. Tom was not lost. His empty shell lay before me, but by God's gracious second chance, he was walking down a heavenly road with Jesus.

Angels in the Sand

*The Lord will work out his plans for my life—for your loving kindness
Lord, continues forever. Don't abandon me—for you made me.*
Psalms 138:8 (TLB)

*W*arm surf, sand, seashells, and some quality family time, that's what
our summer vacations are all about. They all come together at Myrtle
Beach, South Carolina, a place we try to visit whenever we can.

In the summer of 1994, when we were preparing for vacation, I
was feeling the need to use the upcoming time as a spiritual jump-
start. I needed a little self-nurturing to get in tune with God. With
hectic daily schedules, vacation can be a wonderful time to set aside
time for such a purpose.

I packed my angel-making tools and coffee can lids next to my
bathing suit, planning to get a head start making angels for the upcoming Christmas season at the mall. Billy Graham's autobiography
Just as I Am was my book of choice for this vacation. I also told my
family I was going to fast for one day of the vacation, but I assured
them not to feel guilty when they were eating pizza. I did not expect,
nor necessarily want, anyone to join me in my fast. By nature, it
seems to be best done alone.

The day I chose to fast was also the day I spent making angels.
It was a special time of thought and prayer, and I asked God to lead

me to a family at Myrtle Beach that might be in need of a few angels. I made a few angels and put them in my beach bag.

As I prepared for the fast, Billy Graham spoke to me through his book. His honesty showed me that even a man of his Godly nature was human, frail and flawed. Billy Graham recounted times he was away from his family for long intervals at revivals and crusades. At one such event, his family came for a visit, and he didn't recognize his own daughter. Obviously, God used Billy Graham, but his work did not come without a cost. That part of the book made me want to make sure I spent enough time with my family so I didn't overwork myself while forgetting the most important things.

The next morning I felt refreshed and renewed. Fasting brings clarity and sharpness to one's soul. Cleansed, I was ready to hit the beach. Barb's breakfast—eggs, sausage and pancakes—was wonderful. I wasn't extremely hungry, but by giving my taste buds a break, they seemed to regenerate. I could pick out nuances of flavor I had spent years overlooking. It was like taking a deep breath after a summer storm.

As I always do, I went down to the beach early and planted the umbrella, marking our spot for the day. I came back to the room and grabbed my book and the beach bag, making sure the angels were inside, and told the rest of my family I'd meet them on the beach.

As I got to the pool area, I saw a woman reading a book that looked familiar. As I got closer I saw it was Billy Graham's book— the same one I was reading. Was God trying to give me a sign? Passing by without asking about the book was out of the question. I approached her and asked what she thought of the book. We briefly discussed it, and then I asked about her family and if they were on vacation. She said she was with her children and her husband couldn't get away from his job. Immediately, I thought about what I had read in the book about Billy Graham spending too little time with his family. As we spoke more, it was clear their marriage was a bit shaky due to how much he worked.

"You're not going to believe this," I said, "but I have something to give you. I made something special for a family, and I asked God to choose the family for me. I believe God had your family in mind and I hope I have enough gifts. How many children do you have?"

"I have three children and my husband is at home, so there are five of us all together," she said.

I had no idea how many angels I had made the day before because I had been caught up in the tranquility of my fasting. Numbers and counting did not seem important yesterday, but I would be embarrassed if I didn't have enough for the entire family. I rummaged through the beach bag and pulled out all of the angels I had made. There happened to be five of them. I thought to myself, "God, you did it again."

I asked her to take one angel home for her husband so hopefully it would encourage him to search beyond his job for stability. I told her I would pray for her and her family. She thanked me and told me she would be praying, too.

One of her children came up while we were talking, and I gave him an angel. The excitement he showed for the little metal coffee can lid shaped into an angel was worth every second I spent making it. I only wished his father was there to see and feel that excitement. Maybe some day I will see the family again at Myrtle Beach, a family of five walking on the sand and hearing the roar of the surf, so no one will have to say, "I wish Dad was here with us."

Park City Perspective

Are not all angels ministering spirits sent to
serve those who will inherit salvation?
Hebrews 1:14 (NIV)

$\mathcal{P}$ark City Center is like any other big mall. It's a constant hum of activity; a quintessential example of free enterprise, capitalism and commercialism; a symbol of our very country—of how much I have, and of how much I've taken for granted. One Christmas on an angel mission to the mall, I met a Bosnian refugee family, only one of whom spoke limited English. I watched them struggle to order a soft pretzel and a soda, count their money and receive the correct change. I saw a combination of fear and wonder in their faces, but what struck me most was the way they smiled.

The man who spoke English told me he recently lost everything, including his wife and children, a brother and all of his possessions. He had every right to be angry with the world, but he smiled. He was cheerful, obviously relishing his role of translator and under-standing all too well that life goes on. He told me the family he was living with fled from the war in Bosnia in the early 1990s before the killing started. Through the generosity of a sponsoring church, these people had a roof over their heads and clothes on their backs, but little else. They were taking classes to learn English, and to start a new life. At this point all they knew was sorrow and gratitude, which was an odd combination.

With our limited conversation, I tried to share some of my stories. I wanted to let them know they were chosen by God to receive this gift, and that He loved them. I gave an angel to each of them. The children opened the gifts, clearly treasuring those shaped pieces of metal. The girls cradled the angels as if they were dolls received on Christmas morning. The boys lifted them up and spun them like whirligigs. Maybe those angels would be one of the few things they would receive this year for Christmas. With tears that worked as well as words, the adults signified they appreciated my kindness. We parted with handshakes and hugs, and I watched my angels fly away to help those refugee families start a new life. I hoped and prayed those angels could be a reminder of God's love for them every Christmas.

I sat down on a bench to gather my thoughts and process what had happened. I realized how lucky we are, to have the freedoms we have in America. A family of four sat down beside me, the two young children, a boy and a girl, whining to their parents that they wanted to see Santa Claus.

"We were out here last week and saw Santa," the father said gruffly. "We're not going again."

"But I want to see Santa Claus!" the two children whined. The parents took turns telling the kids they were not going to see Santa when they could break away form their own arguing.

This was not a once and done conversation between the parents. Ten minutes later the yelling and bickering were only creating more tension for the family. I said to the parents, "Do you mind if I give your children a gift?"

The father gruffly replied he didn't mind.

I reached into my bag and handed both children a wrapped angel.

The girl looked up at me and said, "Hey Santa, how comes this doesn't have my name on it?"

"Honey, I'm not Santa Claus," I said. "I come out to the mall and give out these gifts to special children like you, and talk to you about Jesus."

"Oh, OK," she said.

The children opened the wrapping paper and were captivated by the angels. They quieted down, admiring their simple form. Their parents were still fighting and arguing loudly. The children were finally at peace, and the parents couldn't see it. God has a way of nurturing his children.

God tries to keep me attuned to what He wants me to do. On another evening at the mall, a woman caught my eye. She was wearing dark lipstick, sunglasses and a black leather jacket. Her hair was tied back with a bandana, and her lips, nose and ears were pierced multiple times. She was intimidating, to say the least. My first thought was that I was glad that someone was sitting next to me. I didn't want to have to talk with this woman alone. It had been a long night and she did not look like she would be receptive to God's word.

The man beside me got up and left. She sat down immediately. I promised God I would share with the next person that sat down, so I handed her a gift. I told her God loved her, and she was a very special person.

She took off her sunglasses and laughed. She proceeded to tell me she was a youth leader for a church group. They were at the mall playing a game, where the kids try to find all of their leaders who were disguised throughout the mall.

She assured me this was not her normal attire and the piercings were fake. As we shared stories, she told me even the parents of some of the children from the church did not recognize her. None of the kids had found her either.

It was a light-hearted moment of my ministry, but it reinforced some valuable lessons. First, I should not be the one to judge people by their looks or their attire. Second, God will always lead the right people to me. Talking to her was the boost I needed more than anything else that evening.

Flying with Angels

*Do not forget to entertain strangers, for by so doing some people
have entertained angels without knowing it.*
Hebrews 13:2 (NIV)

$\mathcal{M}$eeting new people at the mall has gotten easier over the years
since the encounter with the young woman in the wheelchair. I've
learned that God will direct and guide me to people, but He will also
direct and guide others to me. This is when we truly grasp we are
dealing with a living, working God. Sometimes I don't have to look
hard for people that God has selected me to talk to. Often, they sit
down nearby and give me the cues I need to follow.

Once, I overheard a conversation between an elderly woman in
a wheelchair and her daughter as they were sitting behind me on a
bench at the mall. Apparently, the daughter had finally convinced
her mother to leave the house. She had rented a wheelchair and
parked her mother in the center of the mall where she could watch
people go by. After a conversation about how good it was for her
mother to be out of the house, the daughter left to do some Christmas shopping for her son.

I saw an opportunity so I turned around to talk with the elderly
woman. If a person can look uneasy and relieved at the same time, she
did. She was uneasy about the commotion of the mall but relieved she

was once again a part, albeit passively, of the hustle and bustle.

"Sorry if I was eavesdropping, but it sounds like you haven't been out here for awhile," I said.

"No, I haven't been out of my house for more than two years now," she replied, "and my daughter insisted we were going to the mall today, so here I am."

I found out she had been going through waves of depression. Her husband and brother died within a short time of each other, and life was rather meaningless to her.

"I guess you're wondering about these dark glasses," she said, pointing to the sunglasses she was wearing.

"I hadn't really noticed," I said.

"Well," she started, "I fell the other day, and I have a black eye, and I didn't want anyone to notice."

I had to stifle a laugh. Even though she didn't want people to notice her black eye, she wanted to be sure I noticed the sunglasses and the reason why she was wearing them. I wondered which would draw more attention.

As we continued talking, she mentioned her other daughter, who lived in Florida, wanted her to fly down for a visit.

"You really should go down and see her," I said.

"No, I can't," she said. "I'm afraid of flying."

"I'll pray God will take the fear of flying away from you, and for safety on your trip. There's nothing to it. You can do this."

I gave her one of my gifts, and she said she really appreciated it. As she opened it up, I told her the angel would look over her as she was flying to Florida. She laughed a little as I continued, "I'm glad you came out here tonight, and I had a chance to talk to you and give you this gift. It's not good to stay in your house and think about all the negative things that could happen. You have a lot to live for. I know you can still laugh."

"Oh, you're just being nice," she said.

"No, I think you do have a lot to live for," I said. "Think of it this way: Your first day out of the house and you get to meet me. That's a whole lot better than sitting around your house. You have a lot of energy and love to give to your family."

She laughed again. We talked until her daughter came back, and I watched her being wheeled down the corridor. I have no idea whether she ever took the trip to Florida or whether she decided to get out of the house more often, but I hoped and prayed my angel would be a constant reminder to her we all have so much to live for, no matter how old or young, how fragile or how healthy we are. I hoped those angel wings would help her fly.

Wheelchair and Whiskey

In the same way, I tell you, there is rejoicing in the presence
of the angels of God over one sinner who repents.
Luke 15:10 (NIV)

$\mathcal{O}$ne day in 1996, I received a telephone call from a worried acquaintance. She wanted my help in dealing with a friend from work. This friend had a physical disability that kept him in a wheelchair. He had been caught dealing drugs at work, and he lost his job. On top of that, he was an alcoholic. She was concerned he was depressed and might try to take his life.

"Will you go talk to him, Karl?" she said. "I know you have dealt with young people in the past, and I think he needs someone to talk to."

"Does he want me to talk with him?" I asked. "I'd love to talk with him if he really wants me to."

She checked with him, and he didn't mind. I arranged to meet with him that evening at his apartment. As I walked inside, the smell of cigarettes, whiskey and beer filled my nostrils. He was drunk, but that didn't matter to me. I still wanted to help him.

"Let's get to the point," I said. "You need help."

"I know I do," he stammered.

"There are programs that can help you. You can't do this alone right now. I know of one program called Teen Challenge. I have the papers for you to look at. It's a year-long program. . ."

"I can't go through a year-long program," he interrupted.

"What are you going to do with your extra time?" I asked. "Sit here and continue with this lifestyle?"

With a drunken laugh he said, "Yeah, I know, I have to do something."

"I'll leave the papers here, and you can let me know if you're interested," I said.

He began telling me about his problems. Among other things, his father abused and molested him as a child.

I told him, "You had a rough childhood. Your father didn't tell you to become an alcoholic. He didn't tell you to do drugs. You made those choices. You're still making those choices. What's your responsibility in all of this? You need help to get through all of those horrible things, but only you, can make a choice to look for help. You can blame your troubles on your father and your wheelchair. It doesn't really matter until you decide to change and take responsibility for your actions."

I asked him if I could say a prayer with him. He agreed, so we prayed, and I told him I'd call him in a few days to see how he felt about Teen Challenge, a recovery program that accepts men of all ages. When I called, he said he wasn't ready to commit to a year-long program.

"I'm sure you know of other programs, too," I said. "You have to want to get help."

"I know I do," he said. "Would you come and see me again sometime?"

"Sure, I'll come see you," I said.

The next time I saw him he was sober. I asked him if he had a Bible, and he said he didn't. I told him I'd get him one if he wanted.

"Right," he said sarcastically, "you're going to buy me a Bible."

"Sure, I'll get you a Bible. You know, I'm not getting paid to do this. I'm taking this time to come and see you because I care about you, and I want to show you that God loves you. There is hope. There is someone who cares for you if you're willing to listen. He's trying to help you, but you turn a deaf ear."

I got him a Bible with his name embossed in gold on the front cover. There was a tear and a sparkle in his eye as I handed him the Bible.

"No one has ever given me anything like this before," he said.

"See, God loves you. He even personalized it for you," I said. "The Bible is what changed my life, and you have to read it. You have to open it up and let it speak to you. My Bible sat for many years before I opened it. Don't wait that long."

"With all the troubles in my life," he said, "I don't even know if there is a God."

"You brought on a lot of those troubles yourself," I said. "Don't blame God for your bad choices. Maybe God is using me right now to help you get your life straightened out. Look at the Teen Challenge program again. I'll be back in a few days to see how you're doing."

The few days passed, and as I prayed during that time, it became evident this person was in a make or break situation. It was now or never for him to get his foot in the door of God's house.

When I went back to his apartment, I found him sitting by the counter with a bottle of whiskey. I prayed silently as I came in the door, "Lord if I am going to accomplish anything today, you're going to have to make him get rid of the bottle. I can't help him if he keeps drinking."

I looked at him and said, "See that whiskey bottle? You can't give it up."

"Yes I can," he said.

"No you can't. If you can give it up, why don't you throw it away?" I said.

"I can't do that. It cost me a lot of money," he said.

"Well, then you don't want help," I said. "You have to take the first step and throw the bottle away."

The whole time I kept praying for the bottle of whiskey to disappear. If he didn't throw the bottle away, I knew I had no purpose there.

Sitting in his wheelchair, he stared at the half-empty bottle, and I saw the same spark as I did when I handed him the Bible. He picked up the bottle and slowly drained it into the kitchen sink. He then heaved the bottle across the room right into a trash can where it shattered. Not one piece of glass hit the floor. He laughed and said, "See? I don't need whiskey."

"That's the first step," I said. "You have a long way to go, but you can do it."

We talked some more, but the whiskey had taken its toll. I gave him an angel as a reminder of God's willingness to help him, and I left.

He was so close to enrolling in the program. He wanted help, but whether it was fear or pride, he never committed to a program. Out in my car, I cried and prayed, "You know, Lord, we tried. We planted a seed, and gave him the opportunity to help himself. Maybe now isn't the right time, but please, Lord, keep working on his heart. Let him open the Bible and get to know you in a personal way."

He moved to Pittsburgh, Pa., shortly after my last visit, and I haven't heard from him since. I can only hope and pray the Bible and angel went with him. To this day, I can still see the whiskey bottle sailing across the room. That sign, that purified toss, has continued to leave me with a hint of hope that he was open to God's love.

Angel Wings and Tire Treads

For he will command his angels concerning
you to guard you in all your ways.
Psalms 91:11 (NIV)

God never wants us to get too comfortable. He never wants us to say we have done our share and we deserve a break. Like an old faithful workhorse, he wants us standing by whenever He calls. Sometimes, we cannot hear Him.

One Sunday after church, my family decided to make our own lunches, and I had made the perfect sandwich. It had turkey and tomato with lettuce and onion, a touch of mayo and horseradish. I heated up my favorite soup and sat down with my masterpiece in front of me. Then the doorbell rang. My daughter Lindsey answered it, and as I was about to sink my teeth into my sandwich, she came to me and told me a woman was at the door who needed help. Her car had broken down.

"Wait until I finish my lunch, and I'll go see what I can do," I said.

Lindsey glared at me and I could tell by her eyes I said the wrong thing.

"Dad, she needs help now. What are you going to do, make her wait while you sit in here and eat lunch?"

Lunch could wait. I gave my sandwich a longing look as I stood up from the table. I looked out the door and saw a car sitting in my driveway facing the road with a missing front left tire. I was perplexed. I walked out to the woman, who was with another woman and two children, and I asked them what happened. She said she had felt the car wobble as she drove past my driveway and decided she should turn around and head back home. Something didn't seem right to her. As she backed into the driveway and began pulling out, the front end of the car fell down.

"Where's the tire?" I asked.

"I don't know," she said. "I don't know where it went."

I looked all around. Another motorist stopped to help search for the tire. Finally, the Good Samaritan motorist found the lost tire across the road in a ditch. He carried it back, and amazingly, there was nothing wrong with the car or the tire. Apparently, the woman's husband had been working on the car, and he had forgotten to put the lug nuts on the wheel.

We borrowed one lug nut from each of the other three wheels to secure the lost tire. "This will get you home," I said, "but I wouldn't drive too far like this before you get those other lug nuts on."

"Don't worry," the woman said, "we're going straight home now. This was scary enough."

"I can't believe how lucky you are," I said. "The tire could have flown off at any time."

"We were going 50 miles an hour," she said. "I can't believe how lucky we are either."

The woman started to swear several times but always caught herself and apologized. I'm not sure what prompted her to keep apologizing. I hadn't done anything to indicate it bothered me, but I appreciated her effort. Her car was a wreck, but not from the tire falling off. It was ripped apart inside. There wasn't a backseat. The kids were sitting on boxes. The terrible scenarios of what could have been were endless. This could have been a very tragic accident, but the car was in my driveway, ready to drive home without a scratch on the outside.

"Before you go, I have something to give to all of you. Wait here a second," I said.

I went in the house and grabbed five angels. As they lay in my hand, I remembered a prayer I prayed while I was making these angels months ago, a prayer I had completely forgotten about until that moment. I prayed someone would stop at our house needing help, and that would be my cue to give them an angel. With a smile, I gave each of the women and the children an angel.

As the children played happily with their angels, I said to the women, "Let these angels be a reminder God cares and He is always looking after you."

I also gave an angel to the Good Samaritan. He told me to give it to someone else, but I told him he deserved it. He didn't question whether he should stop. His appetite didn't get in the way of helping someone in need. Had I sat and finished my lunch, this man would have taken care of these women and their children. He was as capable as I was, but this was an answer to a prayer I would have missed. We always have to be ready to act when God calls us, and we should remember what we pray for, because it will happen. God is so patient with us and He puts up with our pride and our deafness. Time and time again, He reminds us of his power and grace.

I walked back into the house and thanked God that Lindsey encouraged me to help these women. I was sorry I set a poor example, but glad Lindsey was able to set a good example for me. As I sat down at the table, I found my soup was cold and the bread on my sandwich wasn't as fresh. But it was one of the most gratifying lunches I've ever had.

Motorcycles and Angels

A person without God is trusting in a spider's web.
Everything he counts on will collapse.
Job 8:14 (TLB)

One hot, muggy day in the summer of 1998, I was driving home from the local farmer's market with a load of fresh fruits and vegetables. About a mile from home, I saw a middle-aged man and his motorcycle stranded on the side of the road. He had the seat up and was working on the engine, but from the sweat rolling off his forehead, he wasn't having much luck. I felt I should stop and help, but I had a lot of fresh food which would spoil in the heat.

With a twinge of guilt I drove home. However, I knew as soon as I unloaded the food, I would go back to help him. I knew he would still be there. When I got back to him his luck had not changed. Having owned several motorcycles, I had a good working knowledge of the machines, but even my expertise was not enough. His motorcycle wasn't going anywhere.

"I had back surgery a few months ago," I told him, "and I can't help you push it anywhere. You can leave it here, and I'll take you to my house to use the phone, or, if you want, you can push it down to my house and maybe we can figure out what's wrong."

"Oh, I don't want to impose. You're too kind," the man said.

"It's up to you," I said, "but you're welcome to push it to my house. It's mostly downhill."

He decided to get the motorcycle off the road, and he took me up on my offer. By the time he got to my house, he was drenched with sweat and in dire need of a cold glass of water. We bedded the motorcycle down in the garage and headed inside.

After some tinkering and calls to local repair shops, it was apparent we were not going to be able to fix his motorcycle. After reassuring him it was not a problem, we decided to leave the motorcycle where it was until he could fix it or haul it away.

After he called his wife for a ride, I said, "You know, you're a special person. God picked you out for me to give you a gift."

"You've done enough for me already. You don't have to give me anything," he said.

"No, you're a special person, and I'd like you to have these." I gave him two angels, one for him and one for his wife.

"I really appreciate all you've done for me," he said, "but there is no God."

It sounded like a statement he had made many times before, but for some reason there was no conviction in the words. He was trying to convince himself, but he seemed genuinely interested in the angels and how and why I make them. I didn't have time to share too many stories with him until his wife came. He showed her the angels, and told me he would call to let me know what arrangements he made for the motorcycle.

He called the next day to say he was bringing a truck to haul away the motorcycle. As we finalized our arrangements, he said, "Karl, I want to hear more of your stories, and I've got some stories of my own I'd like to tell you."

"How about this," I said. "You'll be my guest tomorrow, and in my house guests go first. I'd love to hear your stories."

"Hey, I took the angel you made into work with me today," he said.

"You did?" I said, surprised.

"One of my co-workers, who is a Christian, laughed and said to me he knew someone would witness to me some day. Another co-worker told me you're probably melting my motorcycle to make those little angels," he said.

He showed up the next day with the truck. After backing up to a high bank, he was able to push the motorcycle onto the truck himself. Then he asked about my stories.

"I told you, guests go first," I said.

"Once you hear my stories, you'll be sorry you ever helped me," he said. "You probably won't want me in your house."

"You don't know me very well," I said. "Let's hear your stories."

The past year had been rough for him. He had problems with his concentration and his vision. At times it seemed like his eyes were disembodied from the rest of him. It was like tunnel vision, only worse. Driving was becoming difficult, and life was becoming unbearable. After repeated examinations, the doctors suggested some psychiatric care. He was too proud to get help, but one day at a friend's house, he lost it. They had lifted up a manhole cover to check for a sewer leak, and inside there was nothing but darkness and spiders. He literally lost his mind. It took an ambulance crew to subdue him and a stay at a mental rehabilitation center to treat him for trauma. After weeks of therapy, the nugget that had been buried in his mind surfaced like a diver who made it to the top after his tank ran out of air. He could breathe again.

The manhole cover at his friend's house opened a floodgate of memories. When he was a young child, his father sometimes came home drunk. On those occasions he beat and abused anything in sight, including his children. When his mother knew her husband would be coming home in unstable condition, she would take her children to the basement and put them behind a small door that led to a crawl space. There was nothing in there but spiders and empty darkness. Often, they would have to stay hidden there for hours, feeling the spiders crawl around their arms and necks and not daring to scream, waiting for their father to end his rampage and fall asleep.

He had suppressed these memories for so long, he was like a pressure cooker waiting to explode. After much time and therapy, he was able to get his life back together, but he still had an intense fear of spiders. He also told me his wife had severe medical problems in the past year.

"See," I reminded him, "God picked you to receive those angels. He's using me to try to help you. I didn't know about any of your troubles when I stopped to help you the other day."

"Well, Karl, I don't believe in God," he said. "This is all a coincidence. When I die I'm going to hell because my friends are there, but I really would like to hear your stories now."

I didn't mention the lack of logic in his statement. If there is no God, how is there a hell? It was obvious he was at least starting to believe or starting to want to believe, but it wasn't going to happen quite yet.

He and I had a lot in common. Neither of us had an earthly father that could physically be there for us. I had been where he was now spiritually, searching, questioning and trying to find answers in a hard, cruel world. As soon as he realized I was not a flame-throwing evangelist but an ordinary person who enjoyed riding motorcycles like him, we could talk easily. I told him my stories. I started with my mom's funeral and the signs I asked for from God. I shared the stories of my mom and sister's vision, and of the angel picture I found taped to the door at my mom's house. I did not know why, but I needed to talk about angels.

"I still don't believe in God, Karl," he admitted, "but I really appreciate all you've done for me. Thanks for being so kind."

As he was getting ready to leave, I gave him another gift, a new Bible.

"You know, Karl, most people don't give gifts like this all the time. You're too nice," he said with a grin.

"I want you to have this. It has a lot of answers in it, but you have to take the time to read it."

I saw the worried look on his face as he looked at the motorcycle strapped to the back of the truck. He was hoping to make it home with the truck, the motorcycle and himself all intact.

"Do you mind if I pray for your safety?" I asked.

"I would appreciate it, Karl," he said.

Two minutes earlier, he had told me he did not believe in God, but he wanted my prayer. I prayed for his safety, and I told him to call me as soon as he got home.

When the phone rang half an hour later, I answered with, "Hey, I'm glad you got home safely."

"How did you know it would be me calling?" He asked.

"You said you'd call, and you got your first prayer answered by making it home with no problems," I reminded him.

"I had no problems at all. The motorcycle didn't move at all on the way home. Thanks again. I want to tell you I'm going to take the Bible to work with me and start reading it."

My mind flashed back to my work breaks with my Bible after my mom's death. "That's a great idea. I encourage you to start with the book of James. I think it's a good introduction for new readers."

"Karl," he said, "I still don't believe there is a God, but I would like to hear more of your stories. Would you and your wife come to our house next weekend? There's something else I haven't told you."

We drove to their home, about 25 miles from Lancaster the

following weekend and spent an evening in their basement, which they had remodeled in nostalgic 1950s decor. Sitting on the bar was a beautiful brass angel he had bought at a garage sale. Angels kept popping into his life. We talked about what he was reading in the Bible and if he asked Jesus into his heart, but he wasn't getting closer to accepting Jesus as his personal Savior.

Then he told us about Delbert McClinton's song "Sending me Angels." He had been playing this country song over and over again for the past month or so. His wife said his obsession with the song was driving her crazy. He played it for us and showed us the music video that went with the song. He played it very loud and sang along. He not only knew the words, they had become a part of him. He could even act out parts of the video.

> Walked down to the river stood on the shore.
> Seems like the devil's always trying to get in my door.
> just when I thought I couldn't take any more
> Here he comes again, my friend.
>
> He keeps sending me angels from up on high.
> He keeps sending me angels to teach me to fly.
> He keeps sending me angels sweet and true.
> He keeps sending me angels just like you.
>
> As I stand on this mountain face to the wind
> amazed at the number of times we all sinned.
> The countless enemies that should have been friends
> Oh here he comes again
>
> He keeps sending me angels. Here they come a flyin'
> He keeps sending me angels to keep me from cryin'

He keeps sending me angels so I won't be blue.
He keeps sending me angels just like you.

Some say that it's comin'. I say it's already here.
The love that's among us through the joy and the fear.
When I look in your eyes everything is so clear.
My friend, here he comes again.

He keeps sending me angels from up on high.
He keeps sending me angels to teach me to fly.
He keeps sending me angels sweet and true.
He keeps sending me angels just like you.

Jerry Lynn Williams
Frankie Miller

Barb and I were almost in tears as we watched him sing the song. God had been preparing him for my angels long before I had ever met this man. God was giving him so many signs, but they were still only coincidences to him. Why was I the one to help him along the road? Why was he captivated by a song about angels? Why did a person who thought he should go to hell have a brass angel sitting on his bar? I thought to myself, "God is speaking to him and he doesn't hear Him."

But then I had a realization. This was all so new to him. Sure, I had not been much of a believer when I was young, but I had gone to church, and I had a mom who constantly prayed for me. He had a father who beat him and a mother who lived in fear of her husband. He had never been to a church, and the Bible I gave him was the first Bible he ever held. God used me again to help plant a seed.

This man was like a confused adolescent. He didn't know what to expect from the world, or from God, and he did not know what they expected from him. When he grows out of his adolescence, he will be a powerful man with powerful stories to tell. He is in the process of making them. I hope he will always be willing to share his story with the world. When we left their house I felt sure the seed I had planted would someday break ground and begin to grow.

A few months later, he invited me back to his house. While driving there, a song came on the radio with the words, "The eyes of God are watching over you." I felt compelled to write these words down, but I didn't know why. When I got to the house, I was greeted by a banner that read, "Welcome, Brother Karl." I guess the seed was breaking ground.

He and his wife had a story to tell me. A few days earlier, during a storm, they were outside and saw the face of Jesus in a cloud. They were both astounded by the size of the vision and the clarity of the features, especially the eyes that seemed to be looking right at them. A guest, who was there at the time, saw nothing.

It was the second time in my life I was hearing this story. The first time was from my sister over Easter dinner, years ago. When I showed them the words to the song I was moved to write down on the way to their house, they were speechless. God's mysterious ways are often beyond our comprehension.

IV
Looking Back and Moving On

I saw the angel in the marble and I just chiseled until I set him free.
Michelangelo

My stories never end. Every year something new and exciting happens. God keeps my cup full and running over. I try to live my life through Jesus and am guided to open my eyes and see what God wants to reveal to me, so my stories will continue. Most of them do not have an ending. I seldom get to know what happened to all of the people I have met through this ministry. Occasionally, however, I do get a glimpse of an ending.

Mike Couch, the man from Kentucky, died at age 36. A family member called to inform me of his death. He was working for a church, cutting grass at a cemetery when he died of a heart attack.

I received a letter, years after I gave a woman an angel, and she described her own angel ministry that grew from my gift to her. Her ministry continues in another state with different angels, made of crystal, but the message is the same as mine.

Recently, many years after the first meeting, I got to talk to the gruff, tattooed junkyard man. He was clean-cut, shaven, and starting to go to church. He is a perfect example that all we have to do is let God in and He can work miracles.

I was blessed with the opportunity to reconnect with the man on the motorcycle 10 years after my initial encounter with him. I am happy to say that he still uses the angel as a symbol of hope and encouragement in his life.

My sister, Janie, passed away in 2007 after her battle with cancer. She was a prayer warrior just like my mom. Even after her death, her presence in my life continues to guide me in my angel ministry.

I had one more story to tell before this book could really get a start, let alone an ending. It was to be one of the more difficult experiences in my life.

God's Red Bike

Lord, you have assigned me my portion and my cup;
you have made my lot secure.
Psalms 16:5 (NIV)

When I was 10 years old, there was nothing in this world I wanted more than a bike. All my friends in the neighborhood had shiny new bikes, but I had no wheels of my own. Because my father died when I was a baby, my mom worked long and hard on the assembly line at the Charles Potato Chip factory to put food on our table and keep a roof over our heads. There was little extra money for any luxuries, and as much as I didn't think so, a bike was a luxury for us. My mom always had to say no when it came to buying a bicycle. One of my friends eventually got a new bike, and I asked him to give me his old one. He wouldn't give it to me, but we settled on a price of $10. Where was I going to get $10? I needed a bike. I needed a sense of belonging. For once, I didn't want to feel poor.

At church one day, in a basement room, I watched as some of the men were counting the offering money. It seemed so easy to me. I could slip a few dollars out of an envelope, and no one would notice. I never took all of the money in any one envelope, and it didn't take long to steal the money for the bike. Then the hard part came. I had to lie to my mom and tell her my friend gave me his old bike. After the stealing, the lying came much easier than I thought it would.

But it wasn't enough. I wanted more. I wanted a new bike, and I knew which one. Near our house, there was a man who sold bicycles from his home. He had them locked together on his front porch, and there was a red bike I had to have. It was a Sting Ray with a banana seat. I rode that bike in my dreams every night. Every once in a while, when we passed his house, my mom would stop. She would ask the price of the red bike, and the answer was always the same, $25. "Too much," she would say. "Maybe if a nice used bike comes in…" I had a guilt-ridden used bicycle. I wanted something new in my life, a jewel, a gem I could cherish and ride with pride.

When we would get back in the car, my mom would say, "I'm sorry Karl, but we don't have enough money for a bike."

"That's OK, Mom," I said. "I have a bike."

I knew we didn't have the money and it made me angry, at what, I wasn't sure. I stopped taking money from the church, and even if I stole enough to get the red bike, I could not have explained it to my mom.

Every other week, we would stop at the house with the bikes, and the red bike was still there. I couldn't believe no one else wanted to buy it. I didn't know why we kept stopping week after week. Was my mom trying to make me feel bad, or was she checking to see if the price had come down? Week after week, we left empty-handed.

Christmas at our home was always a special time. My mom would get us what she could afford, but that particular year seemed unfair. My brother had presents all around his feet that morning, and I had two small packages. I must have looked sad so my mom ushered me into another room. I knew what was under the blanket before she even took it off. My mom had been paying the bike dealer a couple of dollars every time we stopped at his place. It was a memorable Christmas full of twisted emotions. I had my bike, but it was snowing and I couldn't ride it. I tried to ride it but gave up before I scratched any of the beautiful red paint.

Perhaps God was punishing me by making me sit and stare at my bike, aching to get on the roads. I felt guilty knowing my mom had been scrimping and saving to get me exactly what I wanted, but I had to steal from the church to get the used bike. It created a knot in my stomach and it lasted a few weeks and then disappeared with the wind rushing into my face as I rode the red bike. The knot would come back to haunt me later.

The memories of those days sneaking money out of the church offering hid in the back of my mind, but they never left. By the time I was in my 40s, I began feeling the guilt of that sin. I had already settled my other incident with thievery—the watch—but it was hard for me to confess to stealing from the church where I grew up.

We no longer attended that church, but we lived nearby. I gathered a few hundred dollar bills, planning to mail them anonymously to the church. There were still people there who knew me. I wanted to make things right, but then I remembered the Bill Gothard seminar I had attended. This had to be done face-to-face, even if it was hard.

It was near Christmas and I was in the midst of giving angels out at the mall, but my arms were heavy when I handed an angel to someone. I didn't want to let the angels go until I had set my own record straight. For some reason, I couldn't face the church I had stolen money from as a child.

Finally, I went to the church parking lot, which was the same parking lot I had run and played on as a boy. I sat and prayed for God to bring the pastor to me so the guilt could be relieved from my shoulders. He didn't come. I was relieved and dismayed at the same time. Once at home I tucked the hundred dollar bills in a safe place and waited another year.

Christmas the following year brought more of the same: Guilt and fear, hypocrisy and embarrassment. Again, I waited in the parking lot, but the pastor never came. The third year, God finally gave me a nudge and told me to try a little harder. If I really wanted to make this right, it wasn't going to be quite as easy as asking forgiveness from the woman for stealing her watch.

I found out the current pastor's name was David Weaver, one of the most common names in the area. I looked in the phone book at the pages filled with the name David Weaver, and saw only one had the word "pastor" next to it. It reminded me of the man from the mall who wanted to find my name in the phone book, and I was the only Karl that started with a "K." I picked up the phone to dial his number because if I didn't call right away, I wouldn't do it. I put it off for too many years, and finally I had the courage to call him. I promised God I would take care of this problem face-to-face and not over the phone.

When David Weaver answered, I asked if he would meet with me. We agreed on a time to meet at the church, and I arrived early. Those minutes in the parking lot felt like hours. Here I was, a grown man in my 40s, shaking like a leaf about a sin I committed as a child. God must have hand-picked this sin for me to make my retribution. The Lord knew He had a lot of my sins to choose from, but this particular sin gnawed at me for years. The pastor finally pulled into the parking lot, and I felt like an actor with stage fright.

We went to his office, and shakily I began, "The reason I'm here is to tell you about money I took from this church a long time ago, and I want to make it right." I handed him the envelope with the hundred dollar bills. "It doesn't matter what you use it for. I know it's in good hands now. I have to tell you what happened."

First, I told him about my angel ministry at the mall, partly because I wanted him to know I was a good person. I gave him one of my angels. I told him I had struggled with my angel ministry the past few years because of my conscience. I told him the stories surrounding my mom's funeral at his church, about the fact that it did not rain for the funeral and about the eye-opening storm later that night. Then I told him about stealing the money from the church.

"You know God has already forgiven you," the pastor said.

I knew God forgave me, but hearing those words from Pastor Weaver's mouth lifted the weight from my shoulders. I could breathe again, and I was floating with the angels.

"May I share this story with the congregation?" Pastor Weaver asked.

"Yes," I said, "but please don't use my name. A lot of people still know me, and I'm embarrassed."

He agreed. "Before you go," the pastor said, "I want you to have some of these pens. I'm giving them to everyone in my congregation this year."

It reminded me of the time at the junkyard when I was trying to hand out an angel. The pen came in handy, and so would these. With each click of the end of the pen, I saw a different message displayed. The first message read, "How to go to heaven." The next read, "It's as simple as," and the next read "ABC." The messages continued: "A is for admit, Romans 3:29"; "B is for believe, John 1:12"; and "C is for confess, Romans 10:9-10."

I was eager to go to the mall. For the first time in several years, I felt a freedom that can only come with forgiveness. I expected big things, but nothing spectacular happened. I was able to go to the mall with peace, which was good enough for me.

A month after the holidays, I received a wonderful letter from Pastor Weaver. He shared my story with the congregation, and they had a special prayer of forgiveness for me. When I read that part of the letter, I finally felt fully redeemed for my childhood act. A few people were curious about my identity, and Pastor Weaver shared my name with them privately. One of them was my old Sunday school teacher, who made the comment about the lack of rain at my mom's funeral. Unbeknownst to him, he had been used by God to encourage me at a pivotal point of my life.

Pastor Weaver thanked me again for the angel, and told me he hoped my ministry would continue to flourish. His last sentence of the letter was, "God is so great, and it is truly an honor to be able and allowed to have him as our Father." As I read those words, it finally struck me like a freight train that, even though I didn't know my earthly father, I have the best Father I could ever hope for—my Heavenly Father. I will always cherish his letter.

When the Son of Man comes in his glory, and all the angels with him, he will sit on his throne in heavenly glory.
Matthew 25:31 (NIV)

A Special Angel

And he will send his angels with a loud trumpet call,
and they will gather his elect from the four winds,
from one end of the heavens to the other.
Matthew 24:31 (NIV)

*O*ne Easter Sunday, I was filled with despair over choices my daughter Lindsey was making with drugs and alcohol. I cried out to God, "Do you care about me? Are you listening to my prayers? I feel tired and worn out. I don't see a change in my daughter's behavior."

I loved God with all my heart, but I didn't understand His plan. I was making and giving thousands of angels out over the years to strangers and telling them there is a God, who loves us and tells us we are His special children. Even when I was tired, frustrated and sometimes feeling like a hypocrite, I remained obedient and found homes for my angels. But I didn't see any signs of encouragement from God letting me know He was listening. I felt empty, like I was in a dry desert. No one understood my pain.

It was one of those times in my life when going to church felt cold and impersonal, like walking into an office building knowing it would be business as usual. I quickly walked out of the church after the Easter service so I didn't have to speak with anyone. I sat in the safe solitude of my car waiting for my family.

Finally I saw my daughter Angie walking toward the car, carrying a white box. She said the pastor's wife wanted me to have this present.

I curiously opened the lid of the box, and to my surprise I saw one of my own angels with a note that read, "Karl, we wanted to let you know we have been praying for you and your family. From the church prayer group."

For years, I supplied our church prayer group with angels, and after much prayer, they decided to give an angel back to me. As I sat in my car holding the angel in my hand, I was overcome with emotion. With tears running down my face, I remember Angie saying, "Aw, Dad, it's OK."

At that moment, I felt God's spirit. I often wondered what it felt like to receive an angel, and now I knew. I was praying for a sign from Him, and He returned my angel to me to show how much He loved me. I had the chance to look at my angel in a brand new light and bask in the wonderful, bright feeling of glory. My sign was delivered, my courage renewed, my prayer answered.

The change in Lindsey did not happen overnight. It took many years and much prayer and patience, but she eventually rededicated her life to God, and He has brought joy and happiness into her life again. We are so thankful. It's my hope that sharing this painful part of our family's life can be helpful to someone reading this book.

In human terms, I'm nobody special. In Godly terms, we are all special. We are all a light to be held high. I am blessed, because God has given me two ways to let my light shine: He leads me through my angel ministry, and gave me the tools to write this book. The timing, the preparation, and meeting the right people at the right time all fell into place. Many times in my life, God has asked me to take a risk. He has been patient with me when I have failed, but persistent with His desire for me to do the right things. In the past few years, God has taken me to a higher level, a level I never could have imagined, because I was willing to follow His instructions for my life.

To all reading these words, I encourage you, too, to take a risk. Reach out beyond your boundaries. Reach for God, and He will show you a life with no boundaries, and a freedom and peace that can only come in the presence of God. In God, each and every one of us is special.

I want to give each person who reads this book an angel. Take this angel and listen to what it has to say. Pray a simple prayer. Ask Jesus into your heart, and He will come. Look at what God has done for you, and let God do more. Then realize there are multitudes of ways to return God's love by nurturing others in whatever way God calls you—and He will call you. Let this angel fly into your soul. Open it there and you can experience the peace and power that God is more than willing to give you. It's amazing how God works.

The angel I made for you is a reminder that God is with you through good times and bad times. The candle represents that you are the light of the world. Keep letting your light shine for all to see. May God Bless You! (Matthew 5:14-16)

Karl Miller